DATE DUE

NO 1-6-04			
JE 2 3 08			
AG 2 5 '14			
NO 2 5 16			

DEMCO 38-296

This book is printed on recycled paper

A Primer in the Psychology of Crime

S. Giora Shoham
Tel-Aviv University

Mark C. Seis
Wheeling Jesuit College

Harrow and Heston
PUBLISHERS
New York

PAPYRUS
Academic Publishing House
at Tel-Aviv University

Riverside Community College
Library
4800 Magnolia Avenue
Riverside, CA 92506

HV 6080 .S55313 1993

Shoham, S. Giora, 1929-

A primer in the psychology of crime

Copyright © 1993, S. Giora Shoham and Mark Seis.

A Harrow and Heston Special Edge Supplementary Text.

All rights reserved. No part of this book may be reproduced or transmitted in any form or by any means, electronic or mechanical, including photocopying, recording, or by any information storage and retrieval system, without permission in writing from the publisher.

Harrow and Heston, Publishers
Stuyvesant Plaza
P.O. Box 3934
Albany, N.Y. 12203

ISBN: 0911577-17-3

Library of Congress Cataloging-in-Publication Data:

Shoham, S. Giora, 1929-
A primer in the psychology of crime / S. Giora Shoham and Mark C. Seis.
       p.   cm.
English adaptation of: Kriminologyah.
Includes bibliographical references and index.
ISBN 0-911577-17-3
   1. Criminal Psychology.   I. Seis, Mark C..   II. Title.
HV60080.S553 1993
364.3–dc20   93-37012
                                                                                           CIP

This text is based on *Kriminologyah* by S. Giora Shoham, Moshe Adad, and Giora Rahav. Translated from the Hebrew into English by Chaya Naor.

Contents

Preface ix

1. Psychological Theory and Crime 1
2. Psychoanalytical Theory 14
3. Trait Perspectives 35
4. Behavioral, Situational and Social Learning Perspectives 56
5. Cognitive Learning Perspectives 90
6. Existential and Phenomenological Perspectives 111
7. New Directions for the Psychology of Crime: Transpersonal Psychology, Feminisim and Peacemaking 134

References 157

Index 168

About the Authors

S.Giora Shoham was born in Lithuania in 1929 and was educated in Palestine. He received his LL.D. degree from the Hebrew University of Jerusalem. Over the past thirty years Professor Shoham has published many studies on crime, social deviance and personality. His theoretical vigor ranges over many disciplines, drawing on psychoanalysis, psychiatry, sociology, law, theology and biology. Professor Shoham has been an active member of the International Society of Criminology, and was decorated by the Prime Minister of France for his contributions to international criminology. He received the Sellin-Glueck Award in 1977. His recent work has focussed on the construction of a new personality theory, developed in his books entitled *The Myth of Tantalus, Salvation through the Gutters, The Violence of Silence: The Impossibility of Dialogue,* and *Sex as Bait: Eve, Casanova and Don Juan.*

Mark C. Seis is a Ph.D. candidate in the criminology program at Indiana University of Pennsylvania. He is currently teaching as an instructor at Wheeling Jesuit College in Wheeling, West Virginia and working on his dissertation. His research interests include environmental law and crime, theoretical criminology, and ethical issues in the criminal justice system.

To Casey

Preface

THIS BOOK is an English modification and elaboration of S. Giora Shoham's Israeli textbook *Criminology*. In its original form this text went through four editions, spanning some 25 years of pedagogical use. The original text provided a comprehensive overview of biological, psychological and sociological research in criminality. Because of the excellent translation from Hebrew to English by Chaya Naor, the sociological part of the original text is now a book titled *A Primer In The Sociology of Crime*. This is the second adaption of the original text and its focus is on psychological theories of crime.

Although a discipline of its own, criminology is composed of a hodgepodge of disciplinary perspectives ranging from biology to philosophy, with sociology and psychology falling somewhere in-between. Unequivocally, investigating the nature of crime is an interdisciplinary endeavor. Thus, studying crime with interdisciplinary tools is imperative, and this book makes no assumptions to the contrary. As a primer in the psychology of crime, however, this book is concerned with psychological tools for understanding crime.

This book presents, then, an overview of psychologically based theories of criminality. Several good books exist on the psychology of crime and criminal justice (see for example, Bartol and Bartol, 1986; Hollin, 1989; Toch, 1986 [1979]), and this text is built upon some of their contributions. Yet, this book differs in many ways from the style and approach taken in those texts.

The most salient feature of this text is its exclusive focus on psychological perspectives and theories of criminality within these perspectives. As such, the book does not delve into the psychology of policing, courts, or corrections.

Likewise, the book does not cover the myriad of psychological literature devoted to therapeutic techniques of counseling and psychotherapy for criminal individuals.

This text emulates the style of presentation found in most psychology texts dealing with personality theory. The book builds on the historical evolution of personality theory in psychology and locates the psychological theories of crime within these perspectives. Our analysis questions the tendency of some psychologically-based theories of crime to use theoretical concepts without providing a context from which these concepts originated. With this in mind, the text attempts to provide background information to current psychological theories of crime. In short, this text is designed to provide a historical and theoretical context for psychological theories of crime and to show major differences between psychological perspectives.

Accordingly, the book is divided into chapters focusing on the following psychological perspectives: Psychoanalytic, Trait, Learning, Cognitive, Existential and Phenomenological, and Transpersonal, Feminism, and Peacemaking. This text gives the student of crime a historical grounding in key personality perspectives, an understanding of the various differences between perspectives, and an overview of the various theories of criminality that have unfolded within each particular theoretical perspective on personality.

Another difference that distinguishes this text from others is its tendency to stray into what might be considered gray areas of inquiry. By this, we simply mean that we have incorporated a broad range of theoretical perspectives, some that go beyond the parameters of psychological positivism. In fact, the last chapter is devoted to looking at perspectives which require us to rethink the way we do social science, especially with respect to the study of criminality.

There are many people we would like to thank for their contributions to the development, writing and publishing of this book. One very special thanks goes to Randy Martin who strongly influenced the text's structure and development. We would also like to give special thanks to Professor Moshe Adad and Professor Giora Rahav for their special contributions to the book. A special thanks also goes to Professor Nanci Wilson for critical and helpful discussions regarding specific topics in this book. In addition, we would like to thank the following Indiana University of Pennsylvania students for their comments and support: Mark Kane, Sandy Hedstrom, and Derry Dorman. I also send a loving thanks to Jennifer Gehrman-Seis, my soul mate, terrestrial wife, and best friend, for her intellectual companionship, advice, proofreading and immense patience with my many neuroses. We would also like to thank Graeme Newman for his trust and support regarding the design of the book, and his endless patience with our tardiness in making deadlines. Last but not least, we would like to acknowledge the late W. Byron Groves for his mentorship, inspiration, and friendship, and for making this opportunity possible. Your passion, labor and efforts were not in vain.

One

Psychological Theory and Crime

AS WITH ANY project, the most troubling hurdle to overcome is the question of where to begin. Because of the structure of this text, we think it is important to begin with a discussion of how we have chosen to arrange the psychology of crime literature. We do not want the organization of the text to be misunderstood as an attempt to present the psychological theories of crime as a linear progression of scientific truth. Our intention, rather, is to show the variations that have occurred in criminal personality theory through conflicting assumptions, and subsequently, conflicting empirical evidence.

In 1962, a philosopher named Thomas Kuhn published one of the most provocative books of this century, *The Structure of Scientific Revolutions.* In this book, Kuhn made the argument that scientific communities (e.g., physics, chemistry, etc.) often present themselves as stable foundations upon which knowledge is continuously unfolding and accumulating toward some empirical truth. Whether conscious or unconscious, according to Kuhn (1970 [1962]), the tendency of scientific communities to present knowledge through their textbooks in this fashion greatly undervalues the irrational and oftentimes chaotic circumstances under which new models of physical and social reality develop. We believe this claim to be true and provide as evidence the historical development of psychology as a non-linear story of conflicting assumptions and perspectives.

This book should not be construed, then, as a comprehensive, cumulative presentation of the evolution of the psychology of criminality. The book is instead designed to present ideas and assumptions made by psychologists about human behavior and criminality organized into perspectives. These conceptual models are designed to help the student organize and compare competing assumptions about different theoretical perspectives of criminality. We acknowledge that none of these theoretical perspectives have a monopoly on truth, and therefore, they should be construed only as aids to understanding complex and diverse human behaviors.

Although we realize we could have organized this material in any number of ways, we feel content with our choice of organization and thus begin this chapter with a discussion of paradigms and perspectives, then present a brief overview of the quintessential problem of attempting to define crime in a way we can theorize about it. Next, we provide the reader with what we consider to be valuable criteria for evaluating psychological theories of criminality.

Paradigms and Perspectives

A common word often bandied about in the present social sciences is paradigm. The word 'paradigm' became popular after Kuhn (1970) explained it as a symbolic expression for defining scientific achievements within the parameters of specific research agendas. A scientific field functions normally, according to Kuhn (1970), when most of the practitioners share the same basic assumptions about the phenomena they study. This common foundation of assumptions and intellectual systems that a scientific field shares is what Kuhn called a paradigm.

Kuhn argued that there are two defining characteristics of a scientific paradigm. The first is its achievement with respect to "other competing modes of scientific activity" (Kuhn, 1970:10). The second is that a paradigm must be considerably open-ended to accommodate a variety of problems that its adherents can attempt to solve. Kuhn (1970:11) points out that individuals

> whose research is based on shared paradigms are committed to the same rules and standards for scientific practice. That commitment and the apparent consensus it produces are prerequisites for normal science, i.e., for the genesis and continuation of a particular research tradition.

Paradigms, then, are 'conceptual boxes' — Kuhn's term for framing questions and guiding research activity. Kuhn goes on to suggest, "the study of paradigms...is what mainly prepares the student for membership in the particular scientific community with which he [sic] will later practice" (1970:11). It is this indoctrination and socialization process that allows for the perpetuation of a scientific community.

Paradigms, however, are not to be construed as immutable interpretations of reality. Kuhn argues that scientific revolutions are not tidy linear progressions of cumulative facts which unveil the truth of external reality. He suggests, rather, that scientific revolutions are the result of a breakdown of commonly espoused intellectual systems and methodologies that no longer solve new problems. Kuhn (1970) refers to scientific revolutions as "paradigm shifts." A paradigm shift occurs when old assumptions are replaced with new assumptions about how some version of "reality" works.

When practitioners of a certain paradigm begin to experience difficulties in accounting for anomalies or explaining particular phenomena with their current model – when the conceptual box can no longer accommodate newly defined problems – the paradigm becomes unstable and to some degree contradictory and inconsistent. Kuhn (1970) suggests that when this problem occurs many scientists espousing this model either ignore it or ambitiously attempt to improvise with ad hoc revisions. As the contradictions and inconsistencies continue to escalate, those who are usually younger and not as attached to the particular model begin to formulate new models for conceptualizing the new problems. When enough scientists begin to support the innovative models, a new scientific paradigm is created. Unfortunately, those unwilling to make the leap "cling to one or another of the older views, and they are simply read out of the profession, which thereafter ignores their work" (Kuhn, 1970:19).

Kuhn's (1970) observations of paradigms are based upon historical analyses of what are considered hard sciences (e.g., physics, astronomy, and chemistry). For example, Kuhn (1970) refers to Ptolemaic astronomy, Aristotelian dynamics, or corpuscular optics as some examples of the many scientific paradigms. Kuhn asserts that "it remains an open question what parts of social science have yet acquired such paradigms at all" (1970:15). Contrary to Kuhn's implication, we believe that the social sciences have semblances of paradigms, or at the very least perspectives which are developed, researched and bequeathed to fledgling students of a social scientific community. We note, however, that social science does not possess the precision and narrow range of predictive probability in our accounts of human phenomena as do the physical sciences with their respective phenomena.

Social science, nevertheless, does in our estimation provide sound theoretical perspectives which frame and organize research agendas. In psychology one can clearly see a difference between the psychoanalytic perspective of Sigmund Freud and the operant behavior perspective of B.F. Skinner. In fact, both theoretical perspectives can be used to treat a similar psychological problem (e.g., kleptomania) using entirely different assumptions and therapeutic techniques. For example, the psychoanalytic perspective would look to the unconscious for an explanation of the kleptomania and attempt to make the patient conscious of the unconscious problem, whereas a behaviorist would locate the problem in the physical and social environment and use positive and negative reinforcement to eliminate the kleptomaniac behavior. The fact that both approaches can help individuals overcome their problems through different techniques suggests that a substantial body of shared concepts exist within each to substantiate the existence of a theoretical perspective. By perspective, then, we simply mean a conceptual framework in which shared assumptions exist, enjoy some empirical support, and are believed to contain explanations when applied to various problems.

Our conception of perspective, then, is something a little more broad and a little less precise than Kuhn's definition of a paradigm. In addition, our conception of psychological perspectives should not be construed as mutually exclusive sets of premises. There are several integrated theories explored throughout the text, for example, that build on or combine more than one perspective. Where this occurs, we discuss the integrated theory within each of the various perspectives from which the theory draws its contents. Presenting the theories in this fashion allows the student to conceive of endless possibilities for theoretical integrations. While theoretical integration is important to the study of crime, we did not include a chapter on integration because we feel it is dealt with sufficiently in Shoham's and Hoffmann's (1992) *A Primer In The Sociology of Crime*.

Defining Crime

Before one can adequately theorize about crime, some sort of definition of crime needs to be made explicit. This is not an easy task. For instance, should we consider in our definition of criminality all those who commit traffic violations? If we use the most celebrated legal definition of crime given by Paul Tappan, which states that a crime is "an intentional act in violation of the criminal law committed without defense of excuse, and penalized by the state..."

(1947:100), then such minor offenses as traffic violations, even parking citations, would have to be included in our definition of criminal behavior.

The real problem with theorizing about crime is that almost all behaviors that are presently prohibited by law were at some time in history permitted by various cultures (see Shoham and Hoffmann, 1991). One of the most blatant examples of such relativity of deviance in U.S. history is prohibition. When prohibition was enacted those who drank alcoholic beverages became criminals. Most people nowadays do not consider individuals who have a few drinks to be criminals provided they are over the age of 21. So what, then, is a criminal?

Most people agree that there is some kind of unique difference between themselves and serial killer, Jeffery Dahmer. It is the sort of enigmatic behavior by people like Jeffery Dahmer that prompts individuals to theorize about a criminal personality or criminal type. Fortunately, there are very few Jeffery Dahmers. Unfortunately, for criminologists, this paucity of examples of extreme deviance makes the job of defining a criminal problematic. Certainly all of us have at some time in our lives broken a law that was punishable by the state — whether it was speeding, drinking under age, or simply jaywalking — so upon what do researchers who theorize about crime base their definitions of criminality? Some psychologists use concepts like aggressive or antisocial behavior, which is not necessarily illegal but violates certain social norms, as their starting point for a theory of criminal behavior. Others tend to use legal definitions and official reports to theorize about criminal personalities. Most psychologists theorizing about criminal behavior have had to use as their empirical starting point people who have become statistics because these people have violated currently existing laws.

Probably the most common sources of data have been the FBI's Uniform Crime Report (UCR), the National Crime Victim Survey (NCVS) conducted by the Bureau of Justice Statistics of the U.S. Department of Justice, and a wide range of self-report studies of criminal behavior. However, these particular types of data bases are plagued with numerous methodological problems. The UCR tends to underestimate the amount of crime actually committed in the U.S. when compared with the number of crimes reported in the NCVS and various independent self-report studies. UCR data is also problematic because it does not include federal crimes or many white collar crimes, the reports are submitted voluntarily by police departments, and many different types of crimes are lumped together under one heading in the process of reporting (Senna and Siegel, 1993).

Problems with the NCVS and self-report studies in general include over-reporting, under-reporting, and in some cases lying by the respondents. Despite these shortcomings, NCVS data is technically the most detailed information available concerning those committing criminal acts. Self-report studies are mostly administered as questionnaires to juveniles who are asked to report on a wide range of offenses. The questionnaires for the most part focus on minor types of criminal offenses like petty theft, drug offenses, vandalism, trespassing, etc. It is interesting to note, however, that almost 90 percent of youths surveyed report some sort of criminal activity (Bartol and Bartol, 1986). Furthermore, issues like social class, intelligence, and urban or suburban residence seem to be of little significance when considering criminal activity. Should we infer from this that 90 perceent of all youths have essentially criminal personalities? We hope not!

Definitions of crime and inferences about serious criminal types made from these definitions are still not issues of agreement among many scholars. It is still not clear whether all the most serious crimes are being reported. For example, none of the major data bases listed above include statistics on environmental pollution, health care fraud, and occupational hazards. In addition, when all the methodological problems are taken into consideration, there is still little agreement between databases regarding the "real" amount of crime committed in U.S. society. For if we use only UCR data or Tappan's legal definition we are in essence excluding a large majority of law-breaking activity.

Attempting to define and measure crime is the greatest impediment to theorizing about a criminal personality or type. The relativity of deviance will forever plague theories of criminality. Nevertheless, almost all societies have activities they perceive as crimes and a labeling process for the criminal. Accordingly, this book does not confine itself to any one criminal definition, and the different conceptions and personal biases of the criminal psychologists discussed here must be assessed by the reader. The topics that have been construed as attributes of deviance range from physical characteristics, to levels of intelligence, to human nervous systems, to various acts of aggression, to an individual's sense of meaning.

Theory and Theoretical Evaluation

A book on theoretical perspectives in psychology would not be complete without some discussion of what theory is and how it is to be evaluated. The word 'theory' has many different connotations. Theory is used sometimes in our everyday discussions: "I have a theory about why my car will not start."

Many times we are not even aware of the fact that we are using theory when we ponder solutions to everyday problems. In a vague sense, theory is the process by which we organize our sensory perceptions of the world into logical statements or propositions in an attempt to explain reality.

For the purposes of this book, we are going to focus on the scientific conception of theory. Scientific theory is usually categorized into two specific modes of inferences. The first mode of theoretical inference is called deductive theory. Deductive theory formulates general propositions about the nature of reality, then applies these general propositions to particular instances. For example, Freud believed that human beings had a tripartite psyche (i.e., the id, the ego, and the superego) which could be shown to influence the particulars of each individual's behavior. The id, ego, and superego are general propositions which are used to explain particular behaviors, such as stealing. One might say that an individual steals because they lack a strong superego.

The other mode of theoretical inference is called induction. Inductive theory construction is more often associated with the true tenets of philosophical positivism (the belief that one can be positive about knowledge through the application of the scientific method to empirically verify phenomena). Inductive theory entails establishing particular empirical relationships between phenomena, then based on these particular empirical relationships, inferring to more abstract propositions. These abstract propositions should have the potential for empirical support and refinement. For example, Skinner thought that the only basis for a true psychology was in the ability to predict and control behavior. Skinner started with manipulating an environment to produce a particular behavior and became quite successful at predicting individual behavioral outcomes in animals. From this initial success in particular instances, Skinner conjectured that all human behavior could be controlled by controlling the environment. The idea that all human behavior can be controlled in the manner that Skinner suggested has proven to be erroneous in many situations. Nevertheless, Skinner was a strong advocate of the inductive model of theory construction.

There are many different conceptions and definitions of what theory should do and accomplish in the social sciences (for a few, see Stinchcombe, 1968; Blalock, 1982; Marx and Goodson, 1976). But, despite some subtle differences, all of the definitions seem to use the same basic terminology. The definition of theory we have chosen to guide the reader is flexible and accommodates the various types of theoretical approaches one encounters in psychological theories of crime. It reads:

> A theory is a provisional explanatory proposition, or set of propositions, concerning some natural phenomena and consisting of symbolic representations of (1) the observed relationships among (measured) events, (2) the mechanisms or structures presumed to underlie such relationships, or (3) inferred relationships and underlying mechanisms intended to account for observed data in the absence of any direct empirical manifestation of the relationship (Marx, 1976:237).

Thus, Marx's definition includes three levels of theoretical explanation.

The first level of explanation is the obvious goal of all theory: to clearly demonstrate empirically the relationship between two phenomena. A level one theoretical explanation demonstrates with a high degree of statistical significance that a relationship exists between two causal variables. For example, a statistical study which found that any individual exposed to one hundred violent movies in their lifetime will commit a violent act would be an example of a level one explanation of theory. Unfortunately, in the social world, empirical relationships of this sort are not so easily achieved because of the complexity of human beings and their social world. An act of violence may be caused by more than just a person's exposure to violent movies – the relationship may be spurious. Violent behavior may be caused by an individual's socialization or her/his cognitive processing of information. There are numerous factors encompassing most human actions, ranging from social conditions to biological and psychological factors.

According to Marx (1976), the goal of most theory is to reduce the second level to the first by empirical demonstration. That the existence of Pluto and Neptune was predicted long before they were empirically observed is one example Marx uses to illustrate the second level (Marx, 1976). Predicting criminal behavior in individuals has not been a strength of either psychological or sociological theories of crime, but nevertheless it remains the goal of most theoretical endeavors.

The third level of Marx's definition of theory deals with the abstract and foundational propositions upon which theories are built. Most psychological theories are built on theoretical constructs which are in most cases not amenable to empirical analyses. One obvious example is the psychoanalytical framework devised by Freud. If you slice open the human skull you will not find an id, ego, or superego, although Freud may have thought he could. These intangible constructs are devices to help explain how the human psyche produces and processes a wide range of emotions, compulsions, desires and inhibitions. Marx (1976:238) suggests that third level theorists work far less with objective relationships and more with invention and intrusion. In other words, theorists are often forced to construct foundations for their theories without any direct reference to empirical supports. Almost all psychological theories make some assumptions about human nature which do not lend themselves to empirical proof. Is a human being essentially egoistic and greedy? Or is a human being kind and compassionate? Or is a human being just a tabula rasa (blank slate) waiting for inscription from the social world?

The student of theory must be fully aware of these abstract and nonempirical assertions. Different theoretical foundations lead to different views of human beings and also very different solutions to their particular problems. Awareness of third level theoretical assumptions is important because it is usually the foundation upon which all other levels of a theory rest. Simply put, level three is the foundation to the house, level two is the framework, and level one is the overall appearance of the finished house.

Testing Theories

What determines whether a theory is good or bad? Testability is the most common answer to this question: can the theory be put into empirical statements which are measurable and verifiable? (Stinchcombe, 1968; Blalock, 1969; Marx, 1976; Goodson and Morgan, 1976). Although abstract propositions are not often testable, one should be able to infer propositions from them that are testable. For example, that human nature is greedy is an abstract proposition that is not directly testable. It is not directly testable because it would require having complete knowledge of all human cultures that ever existed. Psychologists, however, can create experimental situations which allow researchers to observe whether individuals in a particular situation tend to act with greed or generosity.

Few theories in social sciences and psychology can strive for the sort of testability, prediction and experimental control that many physical scientists are able to accomplish in their research. It is difficult for social science to emulate the methodological and measurement techniques so successful in the physical sciences. Social scientists have to work with concepts such as crime and aggression which differ in interpretation from culture to culture as compared to the physical sciences which have the luxury of universalizing through concepts such as gravity or electromagnetic energy. As such, psychologists and social scientists are subject to a somewhat different dimension of theoretical evaluation by virtue of the phenomena they study (Goodson and Morgan, 1976:208).

Goodson and Morgan suggest that "[a] theory serves as a tool or guide to research by generating testable hypotheses and it serves the goal of helping man [sic] understand the world" (1976:288). They emphasize that "understanding is the primary function of scientific theories and the ultimate criterion by which they must be evaluated" (Goodson and Morgan, 1976:288). We agree with Goodson and Morgan (1976) that understanding is the primary function of theory and have adapted, with a note of admonition, their seven criteria for evaluating theory.

The following seven criteria should be viewed as a guide to thinking about the value of a theory. If a theory is able to adequately meet many of the criteria specified below, then it is probably a sound, scientific, theoretical position. Criteria, however, are limited by their expectations and their inability to take into consideration qualities of understanding that a theory may provide. The most scientifically valid theories will be the ones that meet the following criteria consistently. On the other hand, those theories may not be the ones that provide the most understanding of our situation as humans. As Goodson and Morgan (1976:296) reluctantly and reservedly suggest, "it may be possible for a theory to help man [sic] somehow in his [sic] struggle for understanding even though it rates poorly on...the...criteria."

As noted earlier, their first criterion is testability. Goodson and Morgan state about an effective theory that: "1) it is a utilitarian instrument to the degree that it generates testable hypotheses, and (2) it becomes representational of the empirical domain to the extent that such hypotheses are confirmed" (1976:291). In short, the ultimate aim of any theoretical endeavor is to provide empirically testable propositions which can be verified and thus generate new hypotheses. A theory that cannot be tested remains just a theory, lacking the necessary empirical verification of its relationship to the world of phenomena.

The second criterion put forth by Goodson and Morgan for assessing theory is responsiveness. By responsiveness, Goodson and Morgan (1976) refer to the ability of a theory to change or adapt to new evidence. Oftentimes widely disseminated theories are accepted dogmatically despite evidence contrary to their propositions. An unresponsive theory, then, is one that exists not by its empirical validity but by its canonization in the discipline. Canonization occurs when a theory, whether relevant or not, finds its way into the basic introductory textbooks of a discipline. As the theory undergoes testing it gains recognition. If the theory achieves some empirical support, the authors are revered and at that point they and their disciples have a vested personal interest in the maintenance of the theory. Once the theorists have an "emotional commitment" to the theory it begins to lose its responsiveness to contrary empirical evidence (Goodson and Morgan, 1976). Thus, assessing the ability of a theory to adapt to a variety of empirical evidence is another technique for evaluating a theory.

Another criterion for evaluating theory is internal consistency (Goodson and Morgan, 1976:292). Internal consistency means that propositional statements should be connected and logically follow one another. Internal consistency involves using clearly defined terms and precise hypotheses, and establishing logical relationships. While this is the ideal theoretical structure, it is not easily accomplished in most psychological theories of personality because of the complexity of the subject matter. We saw earlier the difficulty in just trying to define crime.

The fourth criterion is referred to as subsumptive power (Goodson and Morgan, 1976). This particular criterion deals with the ability of a theory to integrate empirical data within its structure, and it has three dimensions. The first dimension considers the completeness with which all relevant data can be subsumed under one theoretical framework. A theory may be able to integrate some important empirical facts while unable to integrate other equally important empirical information. For instance, operant conditioning is able to account for how individuals learn in relation to stimuli, but the theory cannot account for vicarious learning that takes place without any trial and error. The second dimension deals with just how much information a theory can integrate. Some theories may be more encompassing of information while others may be more specific but extremely limited in their scope (Goodson and Morgan, 1976:293).

The last dimension of subsumptive power is its "logical clarity" (Goodson and Morgan, 1976). The point of concern here is how well a theory describes its movement from the data to theoretical generalizations (i.e., the inductive process). Some theories are better than others at detailing how inferences are made from fact A to explanatory proposition B, while other theoretical approaches are more ambiguous about how they move from fact A to explanation B. For example, an empirical relationship between youth and crime does not allow for the inference that all youth between certain ages will be criminals.

Because all youth do not commit criminal acts, it may be wise to look at other psychological and social factors correlated with crime to make tighter inferences and explanations. Goodson and Morgan note that psychology in general has paid very little attention to this problem (1976:293-294).

Parsimony or efficiency is another important criterion when evaluating a theory (Goodson and Morgan, 1976). One of the goals of science is to reduce the complexity of phenomena down to its simplest form of explanation. Put another way, "[i]n its effort to reduce the complexity of nature, science accepts the theory that explains the 'most with the least'" (Goodson and Morgan, 1976: 294). The goal of all theory should be to provide conceptually clear and efficient explanations of the data. Goodson and Morgan caution us here, however, to be aware of oversimplifying data at the cost of obscuring its true complexity (1976:294). Skinner, for example, has been accused of oversimplifying human behavior by attributing to it all principles of reinforcement (Goodson and Morgan, 1976:294).

Communicability is the sixth important criterion for evaluation (Goodson and Morgan, 1976:294). Communicability refers to the ability of theory to be transmitted from one individual to another. This is important because one of the premises of the scientific model is the notion that knowledge is acquisitive, that a person should be able to acquire it through study – hence, the importance of clear and concise communication. Complex theories are likely to have their concepts and formulations distorted in the transmission process. One measure of a good theory, then, is its ability to make sense to people other than its author (Goodson and Morgan, 1976).

The last and probably one of the most important criteria for evaluating a theory is its stimulation value (Goodson and Morgan, 1976:295). Does the theory generate scientific research and is it of public concern? The more specialized a theory is, the less likely it will be to receive funding and become of interest to the general public. One example of a theory that has stimulated a great deal of public attention and scientific research is Freud's theory of psychoanalysis, which delves into the controversial issues of sex, repression, unconsciousness and dream interpretation. Another example is Darwin's theory of evolution, which challenges religious orthodoxy (Goodson and Morgan, 1976:295). These theories stimulated the public's consciousness and led to a myriad of scientific research, investigating the controversial claims these theorists made.

SUMMARY.

The purpose of this chapter has been to lay the foundation for what follows in this book. This chapter has introduced the reasons behind the layout of the book by exploring the concepts of paradigm and perspective. The layout of the book has a two-fold purpose. First, it is designed to provide the psychology of crime student with the historical background of theoretical perspectives of personality, and second, it aims to locate the psychological theories of crime within these perspectives.

In this chapter we also explored the difficulty of attempting to define and measure crime. This difficulty leads to the problem of identifying how much crime there is and just what criminal behaviors should be considered important enough to constitute a theory about criminal behavior. In addition, defining crime leaves us with the problem of the relativity of deviance and the not entirely successful attempt by criminal psychologists to construct categories of normal and abnormal behaviors.

The final section in this chapter explores a three level definition of theory and seven criteria for evaluating a good scientific theory. A definition of theory is provided for the purpose of showing how the contents of most theories in the social sciences are comprised of three levels: 1) implicit abstract assumptions about human nature; 2) potential empirical relationships; and 3) empirically verifiable generalizations.

The last issue of concern in this section deals with how to critique a theory. Seven criteria are offered as a guide to evaluating a theory scientifically. In addition to a pure scientific critique, the issue of a theory's ability to enhance our understanding is also entertained as a valuable means of assessment. As Goodson and Morgan remind us, "a theory may be the model of logical consistency and still be trivial when it comes to aiding man's [sic] understanding" (1976:293).

Two

Psychoanalytic Theory

PSYCHOANALYTIC THEORY'S most significant contribution to psychology is its stimulation value. Psychoanalytic theory has stimulated psychology by generating new theory and by forcing the refinement of old theoretical concepts associated with psychoanalytic theory. All modern personality theories in psychology have come into existence either because theorists have chosen to reject psychoanalytic concepts or because they have felt motivated to extend, refine, or elaborate upon, the basic principles of the psychoanalytic perspective. Despite the many current pejorative views of psychoanalysis, understanding its significance as a theory of individual behavior is paramount to understanding all other modern personality theories from historical and conceptual points of view.

Any discussion of psychoanalytic theory must begin with its creator Sigmund Freud, who invented the term "psychoanalysis" in 1896. Freud was born in Friedburg, Movaria (Czechoslovakia) on May 6, 1856 and died in London in 1939. During his 83 year life span Freud wrote twenty four volumes, enough to fill up two feet of space on most book shelves (Martin et al., 1990). For a thorough biographical sketch of Freud's life and works, see Jones (1953).

Freud's theorizing about the human condition spans a wide variety of topics ranging from anthropological musings about the origins of culture (1946 [1918]; 1961a) to trenchant analyses of the human psyche (1962, 1965). Freud has been considered by many scholars to be one the greatest and most influential thinkers of contemporary Western thought (Gibbons, 1982; Wolheim, 1971; Scroggs, 1985). As a great thinker, Freud influenced many others (e.g., Carl Jung, Alfred Adler, and Otto Rank), who eventually went on to generate their own versions of psychoanalytic theory.

Freud created psychoanalysis during a very distinct historical period and his theories are no doubt a product of particular socio/historical conditions. Psychoanalytic theory evolved out of the Victorian era, which has been characterized, among other attributes, as having a highly restricted atmosphere. This period in history was characterized as obsessed with etiquette and polite conversation, excluding any discussion of biological functions or reference to humans as animals (Samuel, 1981). It is very likely that this social ambience contributed much to the sexual focus of psychoanalytic theory, since Freud built psychoanalytic theory from qualitative data obtained from his patients who were living representatives of the Victorian lifestyle.

The second key feature of this historical period was the increasing confidence in positive science because of the improved ability to empirically disprove antiquated beliefs about the physical and biological world. One example of this confidence is the work of Charles Darwin. Darwin had a major impact on biological sciences with the publication of his book, *Origin of Species* (1958 [1859]), a systematic approach to explaining life as a process of evolution and natural selection based on fossil records. Freud's approach to studying the mind was influenced by positivism; he believed that the all causes of behavior could be explained (Redl and Toch, 1979; Maddi, 1980; Martin et al., 1990). Ironically much of Freud's work has been criticized for not being amenable to empirical analysis.

An analysis of Freud's writings is imperative to understanding the application of the psychoanalytic approach to crime. This chapter will first outline key concepts of psychoanalytic theory developed by Freud, focusing on his view of human nature, notion of consciousness, and structure of personality. Next, we will explore how others have used psychoanalytic concepts to explain and to theorize about criminality. We will break the study of criminality down into four main areas: parental factors, unconscious guilt, oedipal conflict, and aggression. Because of the controversial nature of psychoanalytic theory, the last section will explore some of the major criticisms leveled against it. Many of these criticisms have spawned other theoretical perspectives discussed later in this book.

Significantly, Freud never dealt exclusively with criminals and thus there is very little reference made by Freud to the criminal per se (Vold and Benard, 1986; Martin et al., 1990). Nonetheless, Freud's personality theory and heuristic theoretical concepts have made their way into a variety of criminological applications ranging from therapeutic techniques to basic explanations of the criminal personality (Redl and Toch, 1979; Martin et al.,1990).

FREUD'S PSYCHOANALYTIC THEORY

Human Nature and Society

While the primary locus of study in psychoanalytic theory is the individual, Freud believed the relationship between the individual and society to be insoluble and one of continuous conflict (1961a, 1961b). He saw society as an overwhelming apparatus of social control which requires the sacrifice of individual autonomy. Freud explains in *Civilization and Its Discontents* "[t]he replacement of the power of the individual by the power of the community constitutes the decisive step of civilization" (Freud, 1961a:42). For Freud, civilization requires and is only possible with the sacrifice of self-interested behavior.

The renunciation of self-interest, however, is a great source of conflict for the individual. Individuals must repress egoistic desires and aggressive impulses. For Freud, the core of human nature can be reduced to a dual system of instincts or drives. The word instinct, according to Redl and Toch (1979:186), is a misnomer for the concept Freud was trying to capture because in English drive has no suitable adjective form (i.e., drival). Translators of Freud's work have substituted the word instinctual, where an adjective form of drive is more appropriate. Thus instinct and drive will be used synonymously throughout this chapter for lack of a better alternative.

Eros (life instinct) and thanatos (death instinct) are the dual system of instincts which represent for Freud the "somatic demands upon the mind" (Freud, 1949:5). By somatic Freud meant the physiological or biological needs of the body (i.e., food, reproduction, even death). Norman Brown suggests that Freud perceived the instincts "as the basal concepts of psychoanalysis, having a status comparable to such concepts as matter and energy in physics" (1959:78). Eros, or the love instinct as referred to by Freud, has commonly been associated with sexual instincts, self preservation, and preservation of the species (Freud, 1959, 1960). Freud called the energy of Eros libido and suggested that it is primarily a function of one of the personality structures known as ego, which we will discuss shortly.

Critics of Freud have lambasted him for his theory of instincts in general and have been extremely critical of his reliance on pansexualism—a belief that behavior is motivated by sexual instincts (see Scroggs 1985 for a discussion of the topic). Martin et al., (1990), however, has suggested that we need to exercise caution in interpreting too narrowly Freud's concept of a sexual instinct, and Redl and Toch state that Freud "decided to call all positive affect sex" (1979:185). In short, eros can be directed into many different channels, one could love one's country (patriotism), job, or studies, all of which aid one's self preservation (Redl and Toch, 1979).

Thanatos (death instinct) is a desire for self-destruction, whose job, according to Freud, "is to lead organic life back into the inanimate state..." (1960:30). Thanatos is associated with aggression and violence, which Freud posited as natural phenomena. Freud (1949) goes so far as to suggest that if too much aggression is held back it creates an unhealthy state of mind. Furthermore, Freud also believed that some amount of self-destruction always remains within the individual "till at last it succeeds in killing the individual..." (1949:7).

Freud's view of human nature, then, is one which portrays human beings in a continuous conflict between incompatible desires for life and for self-destruction. This continuous conflict between oppositional forces is brought into some semblance of order through the interaction of culture and personality development. Society inhibits and channels these underlying forces into culturally acceptable goals like love, work, family, sports, and in some cases war.

The successful repression of instinctual drives by society creates guilt in the individual and it is this sense of guilt in the individual that makes society possible (Freud, 1961a). Guilt is created by the individual's acceptance of parental and cultural mandates which often run contrary to the individual's instinctual core desires. For example, contemplating stealing money from your parents to satisfy some base desire may lead to feelings of guilt. Because you seek your parents' approval and you realize stealing their money is not the way to get their approval, you reconsider your base desire. The thought of stealing from your parents creates guilt and guilt in conjunction with the superego mechanism keeps a check on instinctual desire making society possible. As we shall see, the concept of Freudian guilt takes many different forms in conjecturing about crime causation because of both its conscious and unconscious nature.

A majority of criminological theory focuses on the conscious rational component of mental life; however, psychoanalytic theory begins by conjecturing about that which is unconscious. For Freud, rational consciousness plays a much smaller role in producing our behavior than do instinctual forces which lie below the threshold of consciousness. Much of psychoanalytic theory undermines the belief that humans are motivated by rational utilitarian concerns.

Modes of Consciousness

For Freud the distinction between "what is conscious and what is unconscious is the fundamental premise of psychanalysis..."(Freud, 1960:3). Freud believed that our state of conscious awareness is quite brief. Ideas flow in and out without much effort and over the course of one day we will have had an abundance of different thoughts and ideas. Freud was interested in locating the source of our thoughts and ideas and in identifying the process by which thoughts and ideas spring into states of conscious awareness at particular times. Equally important was Freud's concern with how some ideas or thoughts never become conscious (i.e., are repressed) but are known to exist based upon individual pathologies and neuroses (Freud, 1965). Psychoanalysis is a technique for uncovering repressed thoughts which may be affecting behavior in a deleterious way.

Freud based the belief of unconscious mental forces upon his theory of repression. As Freud remarks, "[t]he repressed is the prototype of the unconscious for us" (1960:5). There are three types of mental activity, then. The first type of mental activity is unconsciousness (Ucs) which is repressed. The Ucs is incapable of becoming conscious. The second level of mental activity is what Freud labeled latent or preconsciousness (Pcs): unconsciousness which is capable of becoming conscious. Consciousness (Cs) is the third level of mental activity (Freud, 1960).

The most important level in Freud's framework is the Ucs. The Ucs provides the impetus for the majority of mental activity by housing our most primitive desires, urges and needs. The Ucs also serves as a crypt for the most painful and traumatic life experiences that we have encountered—those which are better left inaccessible to consciousness. Freud believed that unpleasant memories from childhood and even adult life are placed in this vault. How well these unpleasant memories or traumatic experiences are repressed is what determines the mental health of an individual. That is, painful experiences not adequately repressed may surface in peculiar behaviors, neuroses, or pathologies.

There are two functions which can be ascribed to Freud's concept of Pcs (Martin et al., (1990). The first is that Pcs provides memory for those things which we are not immediately aware of, but of which we may become aware rather easily. For example, it may be cold outside, and you may be shivering a little, but you do not realize fully that you feel cold until it is made aware to you by coming into consciousness from stimuli located in the external world. The other function of Pcs is to serve as a buffer zone between Cs and Ucs (Martin et al., 1990:72). The Pcs helps to keep Ucs desires or urges, which may cause pain or conflict to the individual, from becoming conscious.

Consciousness, according to Freud, is that which we are immediately aware of throughout the course of our everyday existence. It is that part of mental activity that entails making decisions, reflecting on ideas, and carrying out basic tasks. Cs for Freud, has a much more simplistic and superficial function in regulating human affairs compared with the kind of control often ascribed to it by philosophers and the classical criminologists. The Ucs is, for Freud, the supreme sovereign of behavior.

Personality Theory

The personality structure of an individual organizes the various forces and impulses that continuously infuse the individual. Freud believed that the personality components of an individual exist as a structure in the brain. Freud explains: "[w]e assume that mental life is the function of an apparatus to which we ascribe the characteristics of being extended in space and of being made up of several portions—which we imagine, that is, as resembling a telescope or microscope or something of the kind" (1949:2). In short, Freud believed that a personality apparatus exists and is composed of three major agencies, the id, the ego, and the superego. Each agency serves its own function, and all three taken together interact to govern behavior.

The id is the most powerful and primitive part of the personality and it remains unconscious. For Freud, the individual has a priori impulses, urges, drives, and desires before any social conditioning has been inscribed into his/her mental functioning. According to Freud, the id "contains everything that is inherited, that is present at birth, that is laid down in the constitution... the instincts..." (1949:2). The id houses the forces of eros and thanatos and serves as the storage vault by keeping repressed unpleasant experiences encountered in life.

The infant is the best example of the id; that is, the infant epitomizes pure impulse, urge and desire prior to social consciousness. The id seeks immediate gratification of the impulses by operating on the pleasure principle; it endeavors to avoid pain and obtain pleasure regardless of the external circumstances. Through socialization the id develops its own mechanisms (ego and superego) which enable the human organism to survive. Simply put, the infant learns through social demands that it must eat when everyone else eats, it must control its excretory functions, and above all, it must recognize a world outside itself which is elevated over and above the capricious whims of personal gratification.

The ego mediates reality (i.e., the reality principle), allowing for the gratification of id's desires, but only through the refined methods acceptable to a particular culture (i.e., superego). In other words, the child soon learns that his/her impulses cannot always be immediately gratified. For example, hunger must wait until someone provides food.

The ego serves both an external and internal function with respect to mental life. Overall, ego "has the task of self preservation" (Freud, 1949:2). One of the most important functions of ego is to provide awareness of external stimuli. This includes the task of utilizing memory to categorize and arrange experiences regarding their relationship to pleasure or painful stimuli. Ego also has the job of determining whether flight, confrontation, or adaption is required in regard to a particular stimulus (Freud, 1949). In sum, ego's external functions include awareness, memory, avoidance of painful stimuli, modes of adaption, and "learning to bring about expedient changes in the external world to its own advantage (through activity)" (Freud, 1969:2). The external function of the ego is what Redl and Toch (1979) describe as that which keeps us in contact with "reality." For example, ego tells us that we should surrender if we are surrounded by a squadron of police officers holding guns on us after we have committed a crime.

The internal function of ego is to maintain control over the instincts deeply embedded in the id. For Freud, "[t]he forces which we assume to exist behind the tensions caused by the needs of the id are called instincts" (1949:5). Ego has the job of deciding whether instinctual urges will be satisfied immediately or delayed until satisfaction can be achieved in a more favorable context in the external world. Ego may also suppress entirely any urges that create too much anxiety or tension. It is important to keep in mind that ego pursues pleasure only through the reality principle; that is, ego pursues only what is realistically obtainable in the external world and avoids those instinctual urges that would create tension and anxiety (Freud, 1949). Redl and Toch describe the internal function of ego as the "obligation to stop my behavior if it is too far out or too much in contrast with said 'reality'" (1979:185). The internal dimension of ego entails mediating id impulses so they keep in check with reasonable expectations of "reality." An individual, for example, undergoing a stressful or frustrating situation may feel strong aggressive urges. The internal function of ego can deal with these aggressive urges from the id in one of three ways. The aggressive urges may be adequately suppressed and normal behavior persists. On the other hand, the ego might fail to adequately suppress strong aggressive urges, which create extreme tension between the id and external reality and frequently lead to some sort of dysfunctional behavior (e.g., self mutilation). Finally, the ego may break down entirely, allowing id urges to reign freely, as is probably the case in extreme acts of violence like murder or rape.

According to Freud, one must remember that the id is all powerful, as his famous analogy to a rider and a horse makes clear:

> Thus in relation to the id it is like a man on horseback, who has to hold in check the superior strength of the horse; with this difference, that the rider tries to do so with his own strength while the ego uses borrowed forces ...Often a rider, if he is not to be parted from his horse, is obliged to guide it where it wants to go; so in the same way the ego is in the habit of transforming the id's will into action as if it were its own (Freud, 1960:15).

The ego cannot hold back the urges of the id unassisted; it must use "borrowed forces" — hence, the importance of the superego.

The superego is an agency which evolves through a long socialization process mostly influenced by parental influences. The superego is the internalization of the values, norms, and morals of society, as taught to the individual by parents and significant others. It is essentially, but not only, the individual's conscience. Freud explains:

> The superego is an agency which has been inferred by us, and conscience is a function which we ascribe, among other functions, to that agency. This function consists in keeping a watch over the actions and intentions of the ego and judging them, in exercising a censorship. The sense of guilt, the harshness of the superego, is thus the same thing as the severity of the conscience (1961a:93-94).

Within this framework, the ego has the job of attempting to satisfy the id, the superego, and reality simultaneously. The potential for deviance is likely to be high when conflict between the id and the superego cannot be mediated adequately by the ego.

The development of the superego is also accompanied by what Freud considered the third psychosexual stage of development referred to as the oedipal complex. The oedipal complex in conjunction with the development of the superego refers to the child's identification with his father as an object to emulate. This complex, according to Freudian theory, is rooted in the son's unconscious desire to compete with his father for the mother's affections.

To illustrate the significance of guilt in controlling behavior take this oedipal example of superego development offered by Groves and Galaty (1993:176):

> Because the child cannot act on its incestuous desires (the father is too powerful and is loved by the child), and because the child's murderous impulse at the frustration of those desires cannot be acted out (again the father is too powerful and the child's love is too great), the child's own desires become a source of anxiety. Fearing the loss of love which might accompany an attempt to act out his aggressive desires, the child turns the aggression back against himself. By introjecting ideals which he perceives to be the father's, he is able to make his own that which he loves. The catch is that these ideals are opposed to his own wishes; by internalizing them the child takes over the task of external repression and erects repressive structures in his own head—he learns to punish himself. Thus is born the superego.

Simply put, the superego is both the internalization of the norms of culture and the basic foundation according to Freud (1960) for gender identification. Note that both genders confront the oedipal complex (sometimes referred to as the electra complex in female children), but Freud's interpretation of psychosexual development focuses almost exclusively on the male child. We will see shortly how some have used the oedipal complex to explain particular types of crime.

In sum, the key psychoanalytic concepts are unconscious drives, guilt, repression, id, ego and superego. For Freud, all behavior is motivated from within the individual psyche, which is composed of conflicting life-affirming and life-damaging forces. In order for civilization to exist these forces must be channeled into socially acceptable behaviors. To accomplish this individuals develop personality structures capable of mediating between their egoistic desires and the demands of the social reality in which they live. The mediation process is aided by guilt and the mechanism of repression. Let us now turn to some examples of how these concepts have been used in explaining criminal behavior.

APPLICATIONS OF PSYCHOANALYTIC THEORY TO CRIMINAL BEHAVIOR

Applications of psychoanalytic theory to the study of crime causation are beginning to vanish. This may be due to scientific research which has changed perceptions about many of Freud's ideas. In brief, psychoanalytic theory may be undergoing an extreme process of refinement in which much of its applicability is being discarded as unscientific and just unpalatable (especially Freud's views regarding women and sexuality in general). At any rate, psychoanalytic theory forms much of the groundwork for many subsequent schools of psychology.

This chapter is primarily concerned with psychoanalytic explanations of crime causation, but it should be noted that there have been many attempts to use psychoanalysis in the treatment and rehabilitation of delinquents (for an overview, see Redl and Toch, 1979; Bartol and Bartol, 1986; Hollin, 1989; Martin , 1990). The psychoanalytic approach to crime causation has focused generally on four basic conceptual areas: parental influences, guilt, the oedipal conflict, and aggression. One of the most appropriate applications of psychoanalytic theory to explain crime deals with its interpretation of the affect of parental influence on the formation of children's behavior (Martin et al., 1990). Statistically speaking, most crime is committed by adolescents who are by law considered dependents of parents or guardians (for a discussion of the age affect see Blumstein and Cohen, 1979; Wilson and Herrnstein 1985; Farrington et al., 1986; Gottfredsson and Hirschi, 1990).

Parental Influences and Delinquency

One of the first applications of psychoanalytic theory to the study of crime was by August Aichhorn. Aichhorn's influential book, *Wayward Youth* (1955/1925), was based on years of practical experience as a teacher and psychoanalyst working and running a correctional facility for juveniles. Aichhorn's observations led him to conclude that environmental factors are not the sole source of delinquent behavior. Based on the assumptions of psychoanalytic theory, Aichhorn contended that there must be a predisposition or latent delinquency which is somewhat innate and somewhat a product of early socialization factors. In other words, every child confronts the world as an asocial being concerned only with the gratification of id impulses and urges. Through the demands of reality the child learns to subdue the pleasure-seeking behavior of basic id urges. According to Aichhorn (1955), delinquent behavior results when the superego remains underdeveloped, leaving the id unregulated.

Aichhorn cited a lack of parental guidance and love for the underdeveloped superego to blame for delinquent behavior. Neglect results in an inadequate attachment to parental values, which are necessary for developing a strong superego. A strong superego allows one to renounce id impulses and urges and provides the basis of civilized behavior. For Aichhorn, the underdeveloped superego accounts for delinquency. Given this premise, he reasoned that providing an environment favorable to the development of a strong superego would be conducive to treating and rehabilitating delinquents. By environment he meant a strong home-like atmosphere of propriety designed to create the conditions necessary to formulate a well rounded superego, those conditions mainly including stability, pleasure and happiness.

Both Friedlander (1947) and Abrahamsen (1960) have elaborated on this particular psychoanalytic approach to delinquency. For Kate Friedlander (1947), the drives of the delinquent are no different from those of the law-abiding citizen. It is the ego that decides which of the impulses can find their way into action and which will be repressed, and in this decision the ego is guided by the demands of reality and the voice of the superego. Since the delinquent's ego is still profoundly influenced by the pleasure principle, whenever an instinctive urge arises, reality ceases to exist. This weak ego is incapable of controlling the impulses, including the antisocial ones, because it does not enjoy sufficient support from the superego. The delinquent's conscience is not yet independent. If figures of authority are not physically present, there is no force to strengthen this theoretical knowledge of right and wrong. In Friedlander's (1947) view, three factors contribute to the delinquent's personality formation: a) the weakness of the ego; b) the lack of independence of the superego; c) childish instinctive urges that remained unmodified when the organism develops. These three factors are interrelated; the lack of an early modification of instinctive energy plays an important part in the weakness of the ego and in disturbances of the formation of the superego.

Friedlander (1947) stresses that the primary factors leading to antisocial behavior are represented by the parents' attitude toward the child during the first five or six years of life. The parents' attitudes may be due mainly to their own personality structures or the pressures a bad environment exerts on them. As a result of these primary factors, the child may develop an antisocial personality structure, and the degree of its disturbance can vary from a slight tendency towards antisocial behavior to a fixated behavior of this kind. Unless the delinquent personality develops early on, Friedlander (1947) suggests, later environmental influences will not lead to antisocial behavior. According to psychoanalysts, the influence of secondary factors, such as the kind of friends, school, movies, and television programs the individual encounters, later must be judged on the basis of the child's affective development in the latency period (infancy and early childhood) and adolescence.

According to Friedlander (1947), children whose emotional development was normal during the first five or six years of life will benefit from their studies at school. Their intellectual achievements at school will strengthen their ego so that it is a better mediator between the drives of the id and the prohibitions of the superego. The school is a province in which children can form a new set of identifications that reinforce their superego and make it easier for them to overcome their childish cravings and impulses. Children with normal emotions will strive for achievement and excellence, and will be grateful for any help they get. The situation is totally different for emotionally confused children. These children's surplus instinctual energies interfere with their concentration on their schoolwork. Because these children are usually subject to fierce fits of anger and jealousy, the social life at school does not attract them or provide them with any satisfaction. They are unable to tolerate the postponement of their desires. School life provides them with more frustration than gratification. The daily frustrations they suffer drive them to satisfy their desires in a negative and antisocial way, which is the only way they can get satisfaction. These children will be attracted to the deviant society of gangs and juvenile delinquents, since these gangs represent their very own aspirations. In their eyes and in the eyes of the deviant group, aggression, violence and delinquency are considered a demonstration of strength and power.

Deviant society, in Friedlander's (1947) view, may actualize the potential delinquency of an individual; however, it is not a primary factor, but a secondary factor of delinquent behavior. Another secondary factor suggested by Friedlander is the inability of problematic children to persevere at their employment. This inability arises when these children are unable to postpone the gratification of their drives in order to fulfill their long term needs. Youths of this kind have a very weak "future dimension" which cannot serve them as a repository of strength and patience to spur them on to future achievements. These children cannot bear to wait months or even years for a desired goal such as a fulfilling career, while facing the daily experience of failure and frustration while working toward that goal. Since they must have immediate gratification, they leave their places of work and are drawn to delinquent and deviant society (Friedlander, 1947).

Karen Horney (1945) also dealt with the issue of negative parental influence and how it may lead to pathological or psychopathic personality development in the individual. Bad parents may produce in a child the feeling that everyone in life is hostile and that life is nothing but a relentless struggle. Horney (1945) called this particular "neurotic" style "moving against". According to Horney, "moving against" is conducive to deviant behavior because it is characterized by toughness, aggression, and a craving for power. Many individuals falling under this rubric, she believed, could be classified as psychopathic, because they lacked concern and empathy for others.

Redl and Toch (1979) caution us, however, in assuming that all deviant children are the product of bad parents. Psychoanalytic theory suggests that negative parental influences only increase the likelihood of deficient personality development, which in turn leads to weak internal controls resulting in delinquent behavior (Aichhorn, 1925; Friedlander, 1947; Abrahamsen, 1960; Vold and Benard, 1986; Martin et al., 1990). The various personality mechanisms (id, ego and superego) are unable to work in harmony; hence, the child is unable to mediate internal and external conflict. The inability to delay gratification is a trait often attributed to delinquents. In psychoanalytic terms this translates into the inability to mediate between the pleasure principle and the reality principle (Alexander and Healy, 1935). As Redl and Toch (1979) suggest, the inability of the individual delinquent to control impulses means that she/he has never developed an adequate ego to delineate the boundaries of reality.

Unconscious Guilt and Delinquency

As noted earlier, Freud suggested that civilization begins when the individual renounces self-interest for the interest of the community. The community represents the standard of propriety which individuals must imitate despite their contrary instinctual dispositions (Freud, 1946). However, sometimes individuals feel some residual guilt even after renunciation of their deepest desires. Pathological guilt occurs when the individual feels conflict between an overbearing superego (the moral demands of society) and the desires of the id. Wanting to gratify a violent or sexual impulse can sometimes make someone feel as guilty as really acting on that impulse. Take, for example, the sin of coveting thy neighbors wife as opposed to actual adultery.

From the guilt perspective, delinquency is a manifestation of an overdeveloped superego. An overdeveloped superego creates tension in the form of anxiety and guilt. One way to relieve the burden of guilt and anxiety is through punishment (Vold and Benard, 1986; Martin et al., 1990). In this sense a delinquent act is really a symptom of what is going on inside the individual; the criminal act succeeds in distracting the individual from inner conflict by providing justification for guilt feelings in the punishment meted out to them. Freud explains:

> It was a surprise to find that an increase in this Ucs sense of guilt can turn people into criminals...In many criminals... it is possible to detect a very powerful sense of guilt which existed before the crime, and is therefore not its result but its motive. It is as if it was a relief to be able to fasten this unconscious sense of guilt on to something real and immediate (1960:42).

According to Reiff (1961), extreme guilt may not deter or prevent delinquent behavior, but may in fact generate some of the most violent and heinous crimes.

Martin et al. (1990) stress the importance of understanding the psychoanalytic concept of guilt as a motive and not a reaction to delinquency. According to this view, criminal acts alleviate unconscious anxiety and guilt by bringing the individual into contact with authority and punishment. Punishment abates the unconscious guilt and provides temporary psychological relief. Crime, then, is a sublimated form of unconscious guilt. The exact source of the guilt is unknown by the individual but it is related to some internal conflict between a desire of the id and the censorship of the superego.

The Oedipal Conflict and Delinquency

Another psychoanalytic approach to delinquency is grounded in the concept of the unresolved oedipal complex. In conjunction with guilt, one version of the oedipal aspect of crime causation asserts that an offense committed by either a male or a female is a symbolic act of either patricide or matricide respectively. In short, since the incest drive cannot be expressed through actual murder of the father or mother, or a real incestuous act, an infraction of the law is a symbolic substitute for afflicting injury on the father or mother. However, for those with overdeveloped superegos, the incestuous desire for the opposite-sex parent may produce immense guilt, and as noted above, criminal actions are often committed with an unconscious desire to be punished (Friedlander, 1947; Clinard, 1974).

The viability of the oedipal complex as the source of prostitution and sexual promiscuity has been explored by several scholars (James, 1976; Gibbons, 1982; Hagan, 1986; Bartol and Bartol, 1986; Martin et al., 1990). There is little evidence, however, to support the claim that prostitution is caused by the oedipal conflict (Bartol and Bartol, 1986). Nevertheless, the psychoanalytic perspective regarding this issue suggests that prostitution or promiscuous sexual behavior results when individuals attempt to substitute a multitude of partners for the initial love object which is the opposite-sex parent. The sexually promiscuous individual or prostitute perceives each sexual partner as the opposite-sex parental figure only to find that each partner is an inadequate substitute for the desired parental figure. The short end of this oedipal conflict is that the promiscuous female searches for her father in her sexual encounters and the male for his mother (Bartol and Bartol, 1986:243). Bartol and Bartol (1986:243) also note that there is little support for oedipal (or electra) conflict as the source of female prostitution because most studies show that over half of all female prostitutes never had father figures. Given this, it is difficult to imagine how female prostitutes could have unconscious incestuous desires for their father. An additional problem with this explanation of prostitution is that male prostitutes tend to serve a predominantly male clientele.

There are many other types of criminal activity that have been linked to inadequately repressed sexual desires. For example, Abrahamsen (1960) has linked pyromania to perverse sexual desires. Erich Fromm's book *Escape from Freedom* (1969 [1941]), Wilhem Reich's book *The Mass Psychology of Fascism* (1970), and Norman Brown's book *Life Against Death* (1959), all portray the perversion of sexual motivation as a source of oppressive government and major cultural pathologies. However, Bartol and Bartol (1986) and Martin et al., (1990) point out the need to be cautious when interpreting sexual motivation as the source of a particular type of deviance or deviance in general, because the explanations are usually vague and post hoc.

Aggression and Delinquency

Psychoanalytic theory assumes a natural propensity toward aggression and violence because of the instinctual framework (i.e., thanatos and eros) Freud posits at the core of the human organism. Aggression (thanatos) is innate and subject to accumulation when unconscious desires remain unfulfilled. To prevent violent and dangerous behavior, aggression must be allowed expression and release. The imagery of this process is similar to what happens in an ordinary pressure cooker. That is, after a certain amount of pressure accumulates, it must be released through a safety valve in order to prevent explosion. The release of this built-up energy (aggression or passion) in human beings is called catharsis (Bartol and Bartol, 1986).

Some examples of cathartic release may be a good cry, the strenuous activity put forth in a sporting event, or the vicarious experience of a highly charged emotional event (i.e., watching a tragic play or film). Because aggression is a constant pressure within the individual, society needs to provide proper outlets or channels in order to maintain peace and stability. Action movies and sporting events are common outlets for pent-up aggression. Providing intramural sporting activities or similar activities of this nature for adolescents has been a common criminal justice policy response to the potentially explosive child.

According to psychoanalytic theory, criminal activity may be the result of an inadequate number of socially acceptable modes of cathartic release for normal aggression. Likewise, violent acts may also stem from ineffective personality development, mainly from the failure of the ego to effectively manage aggression by channeling it into accepted avenues of cathartic release (Bartol and Bartol, 1986 and Martin et al., 1990). Violent acts may also stem "from Eros redirecting Thanatos outwardly" (Martin et al., 1990). A violent act like murder may be a result of attempting to enhance one's well-being or life forces.

In Toch's classic book, *Violent Men* (1984 [1969]), he suggest three ways in which Freud contributed to an understanding of violence. The first was Freud's observation that many of his conflicted patients were troubled by feelings of "primitive Blood thirstiness." Secondly, many patients' personal conflicts stemmed from traumatic experiences "which often included a repressed desire for revenge against past victimizers" (Toch, 1984:2). The third consisted of the inability of ego to subdue aggressive drives (Toch, 1984:2).

Many have rejected the concept of aggression as an innate drive and have offered in its place the "frustration aggression hypothesis" (Dollard et al., 1939). This hypothesis posits a view of aggression based on the frustration of individual efforts to achieve a particular goal. Aggressive acts toward others or objects results when frustration from blocked goals reaches unmanageable levels. However, if aggression is continuously subject to punishment it may channel itself in different ways. The main difference between this hypothesis and aggression as an instinct is that aggression is not conceived as an inborn phenomenon but one that is created through frustration. The frustration aggression hypothesis merges psychoanalytic theory with aspects of learning theory (Toch, 1984), which has yet to be discussed.

Megargee (1972) has noted that Freud's psychoanalytic theory is truly a theory of violence. In many ways psychoanalytic theory emulates Thomas Hobbes' view of human nature, which contends that without government life is "solitary, poor, nasty, brutish, and short" (1964:100 [1651]). However, the mechanism for controlling this natural state for Hobbes was the organization of society, whereas for Freud it was an internal process created by the demands of operating in a civilized external world. At any rate, the assumption that humans are aggressive by nature has origins in Western thought much older than Freud. As we will see, other theoretical perspectives outlined in this book have a much different story to tell regarding this belief.

CRITICISMS OF PSYCHOANALYTIC THEORY

One of the most frequent criticisms leveled against psychoanalytic theory concerns its treatment of women (Gilligan, 1982; Naffine, 1987). The most obvious criticism here is that psychoanalytic theory has been grounded in male norms and values (Gilligan, 1982). Gilligan (1982) argues, and rightly so, that Freud treated the female anatomy as inherently abnormal. This treatment is most explicit in the oedipal stage of psychosexual development. For example, Freud states:

> The girl...comes to recognize her lack of a penis or rather the inferiority of her clitoris, with permanent effects on the development of her character; as a result of this first disappointment in rivalry, she often begins by turning away altogether from sexual life (1969:12).

Freud based the criteria of female mental health on how well it emulated male development, or as Naffine states, "[t]he extent to which the female differs from the male is the extent of her deviation from the model of healthy human development. Difference from the male means maladjustment" (1987:114).

Gilligan (1982) has made a powerful argument that Freud laid a foundation for looking at the whole of human behavior through a microscope designed by males. This argument has far-reaching implications insofar as it suggests that the very discourse which dominates the field of psychology may itself be extremely discriminatory toward woman— an issue we explore in Chapter Seven. If this is so, then the current story about human nature is extremely lopsided and missing valuable information. As Gilligan (1982) suggests, when women do not fit within the male paradigm, men often react by lamenting that women are abnormal rather than blaming the construction of their own theories on human development for precluding female perspectives.

Another criticism against psychoanalytic theory is that it lacks empirical verification. Most aspects of psychoanalytic theory are not directly amenable to statistical analyses of aggregate populations; the theory lacks external validity (Bartol and Bartol, 1986; Vold and Benard, 1986; Martin et al., 1990). Bartol and Bartol (1986) have suggested that many of the major concepts like the id, ego, and superego and the various drives are in many respects too ambiguous to operationalize. In other words, how do you measure a drive or an id? The main purpose of a scientific theory consists in the ability of researchers to measure the concepts of their theory in order to disprove their hypothesis. Another criteria of a scientific theory is its ability to predict phenomena. Psychoanalytic theory has not scored well here either (Bartol and Bartol, 1986). As Vold and Benard suggest "[p]sychoanalytic explanations of behavior are made after the behavior has already occurred..."(1986:116).

Other criticisms regarding external validity have dealt with the sampling frames that comprise the data from which psychoanalysis generates its analyses. For instance, Freud used patients from his private practice who were only representative of the upper and upper-middle classes of white Western Europe (Martin et al, 1990:84). Freud founded much of psychoanalytic theory on this particular sample of people without accounting for the majority of people in non-white, non-Western cultures, and other socioeconomic classes. In addition to this sampling problem are the subjective interpretations of the data by the analyst (Vold and Benard, 1986; Martin et al., 1990).

Martin et al., (1990), however, suggests that this problem of external validity does not undermine the internal validity of psychoanalytic theory. Psychoanalytic theory is extremely logically consistent. In many cases, operating from the assumptions of the psychoanalytic model will provide an answer to a particular person's problem. However, the question of whether the source of that person's problem can be generalized to other similar cases has been a perceived downfall of psychoanalytic theory. In other words, the psychoanalytic model is focused on individual histories and biographies. Since no two individuals have exactly the same experiences, it is unlikely that any one diagnosis of crime causation will be applicable to aggregate populations.

The essential point here is that psychoanalysis is a therapeutic process aimed at discerning problems of the individual. Its terms and concepts may be better understood as heuristic devices which aid analysts in understanding the psychodynamic nature of human behavior. If psychoanalysis helps to make individuals aware of their problems, and results in the cessation of criminal behavior, then does it matter whether it meets all the criteria of a scientific theory? The issue of whether the psychoanalytic perspective is helpful in this regard remains somewhat ambiguous in the literature (for a review of various perspectives see Redl and Toch, 1979; Vold and Benard 1986 Martin et al., 1990).

A final criticism deals with the psychoanalytic view of human nature. This encompasses assumptions ranging from the biological basis of the instincts to the complex interactions of the psychoanalytic model. The sex and death instinct have probably received the most severe criticism with respect to their viability (Brown, 1959; Scroggs,1985; Martin et al, 1990). The word *instinct* tends to make many people nervous, as Norman Brown explains: "it suggests an unalterable biological datum, and therefore seems to deny the environment the power to alter him [sic], leaving him with a fixed nature irreconcilable with the actual variety in human character and conduct" (1959:77). Erich Fromm (1969:47-48), disconcerted with the deterministic implications of an instinctual nature, notes that it is the elevation above "coercive instincts" that differentiates humans from the rest of the animal kingdom.

The problem with an instinctual approach to crime is that it either accounts for all crime or no crime at all, depending on how one looks at the situation. In other words, when we say instincts caused someone to commit a crime, we relegate individual responsibility to the realm of biologically determined urges, eliminating all true responsibility for individual behavior. Instinct theories either explain all crime, or because of their general vagueness in explaining all crime, they explain no crime.

Besides the negative connotations associated with deterministic human nature, there are also the methodological problems associated with formulating such propositions as instincts (Brown, 1959). Brown (1959) points out from a positivist perspective that theories of human nature should be observable. Behaviors which are observable are classifiable, but they should not be construed as instincts. That is, there is no way to empirically verify something like an instinct. Brown's book *Life Against Death* (1959) is a proactive attempt to clarify and elaborate on many of Freud's major concepts.

Freud's death instinct has also been attacked for being antithetical to the commonly espoused belief that humans are survivalist (Martin et al., 1990). However, Freud also believed in a survivalist conception of human nature or in his terms the life instinct (eros) whose primary function is self-preservation. Opposing drives seem contradictory, and for many a dualistic conception of human nature is paradoxical. However, the life and death instinct, or the dualistic nature of humans, is rather apparent in many of our behaviors. Take for example, the soldiers in the movie *Full Metal Jacket*, who wears a peace symbol on his uniform and writes the slogan "born to kill" on his helmet.

SUMMARY

The most important contributions of psychoanalytic theory to the psychology of crime causation are its controversial assumptions, which have led to further scientific research, refinement, and in some cases abandonment. In this vein, psychoanalytic theory has stimulated much scientific dialogue which is imperative for the expansion and accumulation of knowledge. Whether one agrees with the basic tenets of psychoanalytic theory is a moot issue, but nobody can deny the scope and heuristic value to which psychoanalytic theory may be applied to offer an understanding of crime. While psychoanalytic theory may lack sound empirical support, it nevertheless seems to live on because of its broad scope.

Some of the most important issues raised by psychoanalytic theory about crime causation deal with the socialization process and aspects of aggression and violence. With respect to socialization, psychoanalytic theory has raised numerous issues regarding the role of parents in the development of a social conscience in adolescents. In many ways, the family as a focal concern of criminological study can be traced to the psychoanalytic perspective.

The myriad of studies dealing with violence and aggression also have origins stemming from psychoanalytic concepts of aggression and violence. All told, it is difficult not to find aspects of psychoanalytic theory in most major schools of criminal psychology today. In fact, Freud's psychoanalytic theory has become so pervasive that many of his terms are bandied about as part of the common vernacular (i.e., people talk about their ego, unconscious desires, and erotic impulses everyday).

Three

Trait Perspectives

THE ORIGINS OF modern trait perspectives in psychology can be traced back to 1931 in the work of Gordon Allport. Allport was born in 1897 in Montezuma, Indiana and died of lung cancer in 1967. Throughout his life he made important contributions in personality theory, social psychology and teaching (for a more thorough biographical sketch see Massey, 1981; Samuel, 1981).

Modern trait perspectives evolved from criticism directed at both psychoanalytical and behavioral learning perspectives. Allport criticized Freud's over-reliance on the unconscious as the major motivating source of behavior and the tabula rasa (blank slate) conception of human nature held by strict adherents to behavioral learning approaches (Massey, 1981; Samuel, 1981). Allport's antipathy for psychoanalytical theory was based on an actual experience he had in a conversation with Freud. Allport was describing a real life experience regarding a young boy he had encountered on his train ride to Vienna to see Freud, when Freud insinuated that Allport was using the boy to make an unconscious reference to himself. Thus Freud treated Allport as if he were describing himself through the little boy. Allport resented this insinuation, and remarked that "depth psychology, for all its merits, may plunge too deep, and that psychologists would do well to give full recognition to manifest motives before probing the unconscious" (1968:384).

In response to behaviorist learning principles, Allport believed that the individual is capable of going beyond mere biological homeostasis and stimulus-response conditioning to higher mental processes such as understanding, inquiring into meaning, and fulfilling duties (Massey, 1981). Allport perceived the individual as an "open system". By an "open system", he meant that the individual evolves through mutual interactions with the physical and social environment.

Allport's conception of the socialization process was that children evolve through various stages of awareness. For instance, by the age of three, he suggested that the child has an awareness of the body, a self-identity, and some self-esteem. From this point on, the child begins to extend itself outward into the social world, developing self-esteem, image, and identity. When these aspects of awareness are fully developed, Allport believed that the adult personality is formed. Allport called the formation of the adult personality a "proprium," which he considered to be the unity of the individual self through awareness (Massey, 1981).

Once the adult personality is formed, Allport argued "that underlying the conduct of a mature person... are characteristics, dispositions or traits" (1937:339). A trait, according to Allport, is "a neuropsychic structure having the capacity to render many stimuli functionally equivalent, and to initiate and guide equivalent (meaningfully consistent) forms of adaptive and expressive behavior" (1961:347). A trait, then, is a characteristic that is relatively constant, frequently expressed, elicited in most situations, and has a certain predominant intensity in the individual's overall disposition.

Allport classified traits into three main types for heuristic purposes: cardinal, central and secondary. A cardinal trait is one which defines the overall demeanor or disposition of the individual. This one trait usually characterizes a majority of the actions of an individual. For example, if there were a general consensus among university students that one of their professors named Sherman was a real Machiavellian, since he approached every situation involving students with an authoritarian air, then it could be said that Sherman possessed a cardinal trait.

Allport notes, however, that most people do not posses just one cardinal trait like Professor Sherman. Allport thought that most people have a variety of central traits which define their behavior rather than just one generalizable trait. Allport considered the majority of people to possess somewhere between five and ten central traits (Samuel, 1981). Examples of central traits used to characterize individuals would be intelligence, industriousness, cautiousness, practicality and coldness.

By secondary traits, Allport meant those characteristics which are situation-influenced and do not provide very consistent accounts of behavior. For instance, a secondary trait would be something like an individual's penchant for hot and spicy food. Enjoying hot and spicy food does not tell us very much about a persons behavior or personality.

Allport made the study of personality more scientific by positing the existence of measurable psychological traits. Allport's indirect contributions to the study of crime are twofold. First, Allport provided alternative assumptions to Freudian and behaviorist assumptions of personality development. Second, Allport led the way in developing sophisticated statistical instruments which greatly contributed to the advancement of social science methodology and technique. Techniques such as factor analysis and the use of personality inventories (e.g., MMPI and CPI) to identify key traits of individuals can be linked to Allport.

Trait Perspectives In The Study Of Crime

Trait approaches in criminology involve researchers attempting to isolate physiological, biological or psychological characteristics specific to criminals. Trait approaches assume that empirical differences exist between a criminal and a noncriminal. Historically, trait theorists have treated criminal behavior as the result of a deficient physical or biological quality (e.g., shape of skull, body type, sensitivity of the nervous system) or, as the result of a defect in some psychological quality or characteristic (e.g., lack of empathy, impulsiveness, low self control, etc.). Because there is an assumption that criminal characteristics can be empirically identified, it follows that individuals possessing an "abnormal" characteristic could in effect be identified prior to their being able to commit a crime. The underlying assumption is that if criminal individuals can be identified through their biological and psychological characteristics, then theoretically their potential criminal behavior can be corrected and controlled.

Trait perspectives have manifested themselves in the study of crime in many different forms. Due to their diversity, these forms are difficult to organize in a textbook on the psychology of crime. One reason for this difficulty stems from the fact that most trait perspectives dealing with crime consist of more than one disciplinary focus (i.e., biology and psychology) and include more than one theoretical perspective of personality development (i.e., trait and learning). Another problem involves deciding what to include as appropriate trait literature given the focus of this text. There is a diverse amount of research utilizing traits to explain crime. Many researchers choose to study just those traits correlated with particular types of crime (e.g., aggressiveness, impulsiveness, risk taking, etc.) for the purpose of predicting criminal behavior. We shall call this orientation to studying crime the eclectic trait approach.

By an eclectic trait approach, we mean researchers who use the most commonly correlated traits of criminal behavior for the purpose of predicting criminal types without reference to a personality theory that explains how these traits came to be the predominant part of an individual's personality. An example of this type of research would involve a researcher administering a personality inventory instrument to a sample population of violent juvenile delinquents. The researcher looks for statistically similar personality characteristics among the delinquent population. If personality similarities are identified, then these traits can be considered possible traits of violent juvenile delinquent offenders. The only way to know if these identified traits are likely indicators of violent juvenile delinquent behavior is to see how well they predict violent juvenile behavior in the general population of youth. Eclectic trait theorists, as we are defining them, do not concern themselves as much with general theoretical explanations of personality development. They do not ask how the juveniles acquired their identified traits.

The interdisciplinary, integrated, and eclectic nature of trait approaches in the study of crime makes it difficult to isolate a clearly defined area called "Trait Perspectives." Nonetheless, we do attempt to provide a body of literature which surveys the use of trait approaches in the study of crime. We focus, however, more on trait personality theories than eclectic approaches to explaining crime. It would be a mistake to consider our choice of literature as anything more than a framework for thinking about the diversity of trait perspectives and their utility with respect to formulating conceptions of crime causation.

We begin this chapter by discussing briefly the origin of early biological trait perspectives of criminal behavior. Next, we touch very briefly on the use of IQ and personality testing as eclectic trait approaches to crime. Lastly, we develop the origins of modern trait theories purporting to explain the development of criminal personalities.

The Origin of Trait Perspectives in Criminology

The use of traits to generalize particular behaviors or personality types can be traced back to Hippocrates (circa 460-377 B.C., often referred to as "the father of medicine") and narratives in the Old Testament (Liebert and Spiegler, 1970). Hippocrates is noted for conceptually dividing the composition of the body into four "humors": blood, black bile, yellow bile, and phlegm. According to Liebert and Spiegler, a greek physician and writer named Galen (A.D. 130-200) "postulated that an excess of any of these humors led to a characteristic temperament or 'personality type': sanguine (hopeful), melancholic (sad), choleric (hot-tempered), or phlegmatic..." (1970:96). Defining the properties of traits and using them to classify types of individual behavior clearly has a long history, but it was not until the late nineteenth century that traits became a means for explaining crime.

Attempts at distinguishing traits or characteristics of the criminal from the noncriminal mark the birth of positive criminology. Early trait perspectives in criminology focus on physiology; they assume criminal characteristics can be detected by comparing physical qualities of criminals with noncriminals. Cesare Lombroso (1835-1909), who occupied a variety of academic and professional positions ranging from professor of psychiatry and anthropology to acting physician (Martin et al., 1990), was the first to apply a physiological trait perspective to crime. He is also credited with providing the groundwork for a scientific approach to crime (Shoham and Hoffmann, 1991; Martin et al., 1990; Vold and Bernard, 1986;) and for creating the concept of the "born criminal" (Lombroso, 1911). Lombroso based his concept of a born criminal in the science of phrenology, which was a popular part of vernacular in the late 19th century. Phrenology consists of the study of the skull looking for indicative characteristic about an individual.

Lombroso put forth his research and ideas about crime in a book titled

Criminal Man (1876), which consisted of five volumes totaling over two thousand pages. Influenced by evolutionary theory, Lombroso formulated a general theory of criminal behavior which claimed that criminality was a result of degeneracy or atavism. By atavism, Lombroso meant that criminals were left-over specimens of primitive human ancestry. He attempted to identify the physiological features that distinguished the criminal as atavistic by focusing on such things as skull size, facial symmetry, jaw width and length, size of the nose, abnormal sex characteristics and many others (Martin, et al., 1990; Vold and Bernard, 1986). Lombroso claimed that some criminality could be explained by virtue of abnormal physical traits (Vold and Bernard, 1986).

Obviously, making claims that a person's jaw size or length of nose could indicate criminal potential brought Lombroso's work under the microscope of scientific scrutiny for its theoretical validity, methods, and findings. Charles Goring (1913), a critic and contemporary of Lombroso, produced a study comparing English prisoners to military officers, and discredited many aspects of the physical trait perspective of Lombroso. Goring found no statistically significant differences between the prisoners and the officers regarding 37 physical characteristics (Vold and Bernard, 1986). However, Goring did find intellectual ability differences between the criminal and the noncriminal which he attributed to heredity (Vold and Bernard, 1986). All the early trait perspectives relied on the assumption that criminality is hereditary (Lombroso, 1911; Goring, 1913; Hooton, 1939).

The issue regarding physical traits as indicators of criminality did not die with Goring's study. The issue was resurrected by a Harvard anthropologist named E.A. Hooton who severely criticized Goring's work. Hooton (1939) did a mammoth study using a sample size of about 17,000 individuals. Fourteen thousand of the individuals sampled were prisoners with the remaining 3000 individuals serving as a control group. Hooton's study attempted to differentiate between criminals and noncriminals with respect to physical features and acts. Hooton's findings suggested that there were physical differences between criminals and noncriminals with regard to facial features, bodily measurements, mental abilities and types of crime and criminal features. However, Hooton's findings were severely criticized for methodological reasons and for his questionable interpretations (see Vold and Bernard, 1986:55-57).

Although these early trait approaches were important in the development of criminology as a discipline, they have been abandoned for lack of scientific validity. Criticisms range from questioning the approaches' circular reasoning and selective interpretation to lamenting their lack of scientific controls – criticisms which highlight the necessity to explain competing psychological factors and environmental explanations. (For an explanatory overview of the significance and criticisms of these early trait perspectives see Vold and Bernard, 1986; Siegel, 1989; Martin et al., 1990; Shoham and Hoffman 1991.)

IQ, Personality Tests, and Crime

Another area deserving of a brief discussion when thinking of traits is the concept of intelligence. The belief that low intelligence is a trait endemic to criminality began in the early twentieth century (Godard, 1912; Goring, 1972 [1913]), and remains a factor in criminality for many contemporary theorists (Hirschi, 1969; Gordon, 1976; Hirschi and Hindelang, 1977; Wilson and Herrnstein, 1985; Gottfredson and Hirschi, 1990). Although some criminologists cling to the IQ concept as a variable in crime, most contemporary theorists have abandoned intellectual aptitude as the sole causal explanation of crime (Hollin, 1989).

The most scathing criticism of the IQ concept targets the implicit assumption that IQ can measure something as abstract as intelligence (Gould, 1981). Another prevalent form of criticizing the IQ measure, according to Bartol and Bartol (1986), is social class bias. This criticism asserts that IQ measures only the values and beliefs of white middle class society and not those of other cultures and other backgrounds. Some criminologists have asserted, however, that even when controlling for social class, IQ is significant in predicting crime (Hirschi and Hindelang, 1977; see also Loeber and Dishion, 1983). In addition, in their review of the intelligence literature, Wilson and Herrnstein have stated that "criminals seem, on the average, to be a bit less bright and to have a different set of intellectual strengths and weaknesses than do non-criminals as a group" (1985:148). Despite the confidence some express regarding the relationship between IQ and crime, the validity of the IQ assertion is far from established or accepted as fact (see Denno, 1985).

Even if the argument is made that IQ is a factor in crime, no argument can be made that IQ is a measure of something as abstract as intelligence. The problem with measuring intelligence through IQ revolves around attempting to identify all the dimensions that make up the domain of intelligence. Alfred Binet (1857-1911), the creator of the intelligence quotient (IQ) concept, was quite aware of this problem.

Binet was a French psychologist hired by the public education system in France to design techniques used to identify children with learning problems in the classroom. The test Binet designed looked at an individual's ability to accomplish everyday tasks (Gould, 1981). Some of these tasks involved counting, distinguishing between objects, and other forms of reasoning such as "direction (ordering), comprehension, invention and censure (correction)" (Binet quoted in Gould, 1981:149). The technique for measuring a child's ability required that each task have an age level which represented "the youngest age at which a child of normal intelligence should be able to complete the task successfully" (Gould, 1981:149). Each child would attempt to complete as many of the tasks as they could, beginning with the task assigned to the youngest in age. "The age associated with the last task he could perform became his 'mental age,' and his general intellectual level was calculated by subtracting this mental age from his true chronological age" (Gould, 1981:149-150).

The calculation for IQ was changed in 1912 by a German Psychologist, W. Stern, who asserted that "mental age should be divided by chronological age, not subtracted from it..." (Gould, 1981:150). This final adjustment by Stern marked the birth of the IQ concept.

Stephen Gould argues that Binet's IQ test was never meant to be an indicator of "inborn intelligence", nor was it meant to be used as a device for rank-ordering "mental worth" (1981:152). Binet always asserted that intelligence could be improved by education (Gould, 1981:154). Gould argues persuasively that

> American psychologists perverted Binet's intention and invented the hereditarian theory of IQ. They reified Binet's scores and took them as measures of an entity called intelligence. They assumed that intelligence was largely inherited, and developed a series of specious arguments confusing cultural differences with innate properties. They believed that inherited IQ scores marked people and groups for an inevitable station in life (1981:157).

These criticisms put forth by Gould are important if we are to consider seriously the relevance of IQ when considering crime, especially white collar crimes which often require a great deal of intelligence.

Given Binet's intentions, the most appropriate way to think of the IQ measure may be as a diagnostic device for ascertaining learning deficits. Learning deficits may indirectly lead to delinquent behavior via "low self-esteem and emotional disturbances, in turn leading to conduct disorder and criminal behavior" (Holland, 1989:111). Simply put, IQ may best be thought of as one factor among many other interrelated factors like psychological disposition, family, educational quality, and social environment.

Personality Tests

Another application of eclectic psychological trait theory to the study of criminal behavior has been the use of personality tests to predict delinquent behavior. The assumption here involves a belief that criminal behavior is the result of an individual's deficiency or possession of an overabundance of a particular trait or quality which prevents them from being able to conform their behavior to the mandates of society. For example, an individual measuring high in aggressiveness may be more likely to commit a violent crime. A person who is low in empathy may be more likely to take advantage of someone than an individual who is high in empathy.

Generally, the way to assess these "perceived defects" is through personality inventories. Probably the most common personality tests are the Minnesota Multiphasic Personality Inventory (MMPI) and California Personality Inventory (CPI). These are pencil-and-paper type tests which are comprised of hundreds of questions and numerous types of scales designed to measure and identify various personality traits in individuals. In addition to these pencil-and-paper tests is a personality assessment which uses pictures known as the Thematic Appreciation Test (TAT).

The success in identifying particular personality traits predictive of delinquent behavior remains an unsettled issue. For instance, Schuessler and Cressey (1950) conducted a literature review of all the comparison studies done prior to 1950 and found the results to be inconsistent and methodologically flawed. Sheldon and Eleanor Glueck, however, in a study published in 1950 involving 500 hundred delinquent and nondelinquent boys, found that delinquents as a group are more: "restlessly energetic, impulsive, extraverted, aggressive, destructive...hostile, defiant, resentful, suspicious, stubborn, socially assertive, adventurous, unconventional, nonsubmissive to authority..." (Glueck and Glueck, 1979:181). Vold and Bernard (1986:119) have pointed out that while the Gluecks' findings pose a problem for theory construction, their trait identifiers tend to be fairly good predictors of delinquency.

A follow-up study to Schuessler and Cressey's (1950) was conducted by Waldo and Dinitz (1967). Waldo and Dinitz looked at 94 studies done concerning personality traits predictive of criminality beginning in 1950 and ending in 1967. Waldo and Dinitz suggested that over 75% of these studies reported finding statistically significant differences between criminals and noncriminals. Waldo and Dinitz warned, however, that some of these studies had severe methodological problems in the form of sampling, item construction, and controls, which made questionable the reliability and validity of the findings. David Tannenbaum (1977) also produced a similar finding of the literature regarding predictive traits following Waldo and Dinitz study. All told, the advisability of using personality tests to ascertain traits predictive of delinquent behavior remains equivocal.

Another problem associated with using eclectic trait approaches to explain crime is the susceptibility of them to circular reasoning. An example of circular reasoning would be to use a trait-like impulsiveness to explain theft. One might conclude that the reason people steal is because they are impulsive. However, one might also conclude that stealing is an indicator of impulsiveness. In this way, the trait is deduced from the behavior and the behavior is deduced from the trait.

Another major problem with using traits is the difficulty researchers have in agreeing upon a finite number of psychological traits. Estimates of the number of human personality traits have ranged from a handful to several hundred.

Modern Trait Perspectives In The Study Of Crime

In this last section we will look at some trait theories designed to account for criminal behavior. As we will see, the use of traits to explain criminal behavior has been an extremely diverse intellectual endeavor. We begin with a discussion of William Sheldon's concept of somatotyping and end with a discussion of Gottfredson and Hirschi's (1990) general theory as a modern trait approach to criminal behavior.

William Sheldon and Somatotyping. The validity of using physiological features to distinguish criminals from noncriminals has been largely discredited as a viable approach to explaining crime. William Sheldon et al. (1949) was the last to truly pursue a hereditary relationship between criminal personalities and their physical characteristics. Sheldon was a psychologist by trade, receiving his Ph.D. from the University of Chicago in 1925. Sheldon later became a professor at Harvard, where he was influenced by the work of Hooton— the constitutional hereditarian discussed briefly in the beginning of this chapter. Although Sheldon was influenced by Hooton, his work had a somewhat different emphasis.

Sheldon strongly believed that the basis of personality could be found in the physical constitution of the individual. He assumed that psychological temperaments were determined by a person's physical constitution. He is famous for somatotyping, which involved taking particular body types and ascribing to them psychological temperaments. In *Varieties of Delinquent Youth* (1949), Sheldon and his colleagues suggested that certain body types and temperaments were more likely to be associated with criminal behavior.

Sheldon's theoretical perspective is based on the prior work of a German psychiatrist named Emil Kretschmer. Kretschmer constructed four types of body classifications which he associated with different types of mental illness: pyknic, leptosomatic or aesthenic, athletic, and dysplastic (Bartol and Bartol, 1986; Martin et al., 1990). Kretschmer's body types can be summarized as follows:

> the pyknic... was characterized by a short, fat stature. A second type exhibiting height and very thin features, was the leptosomatic or aesthenic. The muscular, vigorous physique was called the athletic type. The fourth, the dysplastic, represented an incongruous mixture of different physiques in different parts of the body... (Bartol and Bartol, 1986:24).

Sheldon, following along the same line of inquiry, created a taxonomy of the body which consisted of three categories: endomorphic, mesomorphic, and ectomorphic.

Physical traits endemic to the endomorphic person are heaviness, stubbiness, and softness (Sheldon, 1942). The accompanying psychological disposition was called viscerotonia, which consisted of a personality temperament inclined toward the love of "comfort, food, affection, and people" (Bartol and Bartol, 1986:26). Mesomorphs tend to be "hard, firm, upright, and relatively strong and tough" (Sheldon, 1942:131). This body type correlates with the type of psychological disposition Sheldon classified as somatotonia; somatotons are supposed to be "indifferent to pain and aggressive, callous, even ruthless in relationships with others" (Bartol and Bartol, 1986:26). The ectomorph has the physical traits of "fragility, linearity, flatness of the chest, and delicacy throughout the body" (Sheldon, 1942:8). The psychological disposition of the ectomorph is what Sheldon referred to as cerebrotonia; this classification denotes individuals who are "inhibited, reserved, self conscious, and afraid of people..."(Bartol and Bartol, 1986:26).

Sheldon's (1940) body types were constructed on observations of nude photographs of 4000 male college students which consisted of an analysis of a full front and back profile pictures. Sheldon's classification system was based on a seven point rating scale for each particular body type. Thus a male person with an extremely muscular physique would score a 7 for the mesomorph classification, a 1 for endomorph, and a 1 for ectomorph, which gave him a total score of 7-1-1 (for other examples see Martin et al., 1990; Vold and Bernard, 1986). The average college student scored around 4-4-4 (Bartol and Bartol, 1986). Apparently, Sheldon has reported a reliability coefficient as high as .91 by other researchers using his classification system (see Massey, 1981).

Sheldon et al. (1949) purported that juvenile delinquents, when compared to college students, were on the whole much more mesomorphic in body type. Endomorphs were the next most represented in his sample with ectomorphs being the least likely to be delinquent. Similar findings were also reported by Glueck and Glueck (1950) whose study was cited earlier for its findings regarding the relationship between IQ and delinquency. In addition to these findings, Cortes and Gatti (1972) reported that mesomorphic boys were disproportionately over-represented in their sample of 100 male delinquents when compared with an equivalent sample of male high school seniors.

Somatotyping, however, has undergone severe criticism for its lack of research controls. When factors such as physical maturation, opportunity, and social class have been controlled for, no significant relationships have been found between physiology and self-reported delinquency (Vold and Bernard, 1986; Siegel, 1989). Assessments of the above-cited studies found some support for Sheldon's classification system, but did so with less than convincing statistical arguments (Samuel, 1981; Bartol and Bartol, 1986).

Consequently, this line of research has been ignored because of its potential for stereotyping and the authors' bias in their observations (Samuel, 1981:192). Furthermore, the theory's inability to offer an explanation for why one mesomorphic boy may commit a crime while another does not is also problematic; somatotyping does not deal with necessary cultural, social, and situational factors.

Eysenck's Personality Theory

British psychologist Hans Eysenck (1977, 1984) has produced a trait theory which assumes that all individuals carry with them a biological predisposition which interacts with environmental factors to formulate personality. According to Eysenck,

> it is taken as axiomatic that man [sic] as an animal is the product of millions of years of evolution, an evolution which has shaped the brain, developed instincts, affected behavioral responses and quite generally embodied behavioral predispositions in the morphology of the central nervous system and in genetic constitution (1984:90).

Genetic coding predisposes an individual's ability to be conditioned to the social environment (1984:93). Biology cannot be construed as the sole determinant of behavioral manifestations, however, because the type of social conditioning individuals receive will determine the outcome of their conduct with respect to the mandates of culture. With a social bent to it all, Eysenck's project is to fuse biological predispositions with the ability to be conditioned under the guise of classical learning theory (to be discussed in the next chapter).

Eysenck's theory may be considered an integrated theory (see Liska et al., 1989) and a general theory of crime as defined by himself (1984). It is an integrative theory in the sense that the theory combines biological functions of the nervous system with aspects of classical learning theory to determine behavior. It is a general theory insofar as it attempts to explain all aspects of crime. The reason for including Eysenck's (1948) theory as a trait perspective is his assumption that personality dimensions can be empirically verified using methodologies common to trait theorists.

Eysenck began his search for personality types during World War II. Based on a sample of ten thousand individuals, Eysenck used numerous classification systems, ratings, and factor analytical procedures to find two basic personality dimensions. These polar dimensions were extraversion/

introversion and neuroticism/stability (Liebert and Spiegler, 1970:135). A third personality dimension, known as psychoticism, was developed later on. Psychoticism is the least developed of the three and has no biological corollary like extraversion/introversion and neuroticism/stability (see figure 1).

The extraversion/introversion personality dimension is directly linked to a biological corollary — the central nervous system. The central nervous system includes the spinal cord and the brain. Where the spinal cord and the brain are connected there is a mechanism called the reticular activating system (RAS) which regulates stimuli and arousal levels leading to the cerebral cortex. In the cerebral cortex, the brain's higher functions such as memory and thinking take place. Eysenck believes that the amount of stimuli the RAS allows to the cerebral cortex is what differentiates the extravert from the introvert personality dimension.

Personality Dimension One

Extraversion	Ambiverts	Introversion
RAS Low Arousal		RAS High Arousal

According to Eysenck, a RAS that inhibits arousal or stimuli to the cerebral cortex produces an individual with an extraverted personality. Because the extraverts have low arousal levels, they will be more inclined to be gregarious, upbeat, impulsive, and thrill seeking. On the flip side, they are also more likely to anger easily and be aggressive. A desire for frequent changes in surroundings and lifestyles is also a characteristic of the extravert (Bartol and Bartol, 1986).

A RAS that intensifies the stimuli or arousal levels to the cerebral cortex creates an introverted personality. Because introverts experience high levels of arousal all the time, they tend to avoid socializing, high levels of excitement, and change. Overall, introverts tend to be more dependable, less aggressive, and more ethical (Bartol and Bartol, 1986). The individual that falls in the middle of this continuum is what Eysenck referred to as an ambivert.

Eysenck's neuroticism/stability personality dimension has as its biological corollary the autonomic nervous system (See figure two). The autonomic nervous system consists of two parts, the sympathetic and the parasympathetic. The sympathetic part of the autonomic nervous system stimulates those functions of the body such as heart rate and blood flow to stimulate muscle, which are necessary for stressful or survival situations. The parasympathetic part of the autonomic nervous system counteracts the sympathetic division by bringing bodily functions back into homeostasis. Under the dominion of the limbic system (the part of the brain that regulates emotion and motivation), the two divisions of the autonomic nervous system regulate the amount of sensitivity that an individual experiences in the form of emotions.

Eysenck contends that individuals who could be considered neurotic have an easily activated sympathetic division which produces both high and sustained levels of emotionality. In addition, the parasympathetic division in the neurotic individual is slow in counteracting the sympathetic system. The opposite is true for the stable individual who has a highly regulating parasympathetic division which precludes high levels of emotional stimulation from influencing behavior (Bartol and Bartol, 1986:38-39).

Persons who measure high on the neurotic scale are "likely to be moody, touchy, sensitive to slights, anxious, and to complain of various physical ailments like headaches, backaches, and digestive problems" (Bartol and Bartol, 1986:38). The stable person is the antithesis of these characteristics; that is, the stable person is calm and well composed. Taken together, these two extremes form the poles of the neuroticism personality type continuum.

Personality Dimension Two

Active Sympathetic	Passive Sympathetic
Neuroticism	Stability
Slow Parasympathetic	Fast Parasympathetic

According to Eysenck, the person most likely to participate in deviant activity is the individual who scores high on extraversion and neuroticism. As noted earlier, Eysenck called those people who fall in the middle range of the extravert/introvert continuum ambiverts, but had no name for those who fall in the middle range of the neuroticism or psychoticism scales. He also had no biological corollary for the psychoticism scale which differentiates between individuals who are cold and insensitive and those who are tender-minded and overly sensitive (Bartol and Bartol, 1986).

Personality Dimension Three

Psychoticism		Tender Minded
Cold and Insensitive		Overly Sensitive

While these biological predispositions are the foundations of Eysenck's trait perspective, they are not, as mentioned earlier, the sole determinants of deviant behavior. For Eysenck, these predispositions interact with the classical conditioning aspect of the social environment. What differentiates the deviant from the nondeviant is captured in this synoptic statement by Eysenck of his general theory:

> Genetic factors predispose [people] to have certain personality traits, which are connected with the propensity to form weak or strong conditioned responses. Depending on the frequency of pairings between the conditioned and unconditioned stimulus in the field of social behavior, and on the precise content of the conditioning program, children will grow up to develop appropriate types of behavior. Conditionability is a crucial factor on the biological side; permissiveness or morality is a crucial factor on the social or environmental side. In a permissive society where parents, teachers, and magistrates do not take seriously the task of imposing on children a conscience which would lead them to behave in a socialized manner, a large number of individuals with poor or average conditionability will acquire a 'conscience' too weak to prevent them from indulging in criminal activities, although had they been subjected to a stricter regime of conditioning, they might have grown up to be perfectly respectable and law abiding citizens (1984:97).

The dynamics of classical conditioning will be explained more thoroughly in the next chapter. For now, however, note that for Eysenck criminal traits are not inherited per se, but evolve through a lack of moral conditioning and socialization.

Support for Eysenck's theory overall has been somewhat weak (Bartol and Bartol, 1986). Passingham (1972), who has probably done the most comprehensive review of studies testing Eysenck's theory prior to 1972, found many methodological problems as well as little support for the prediction that extraversion is more likely to lead to criminal behavior. There have been several studies since Passingham's (1972) review that have also found little support for major differences between criminals and noncriminals regarding the extraversion scale (Allsopp, 1976; Feldman, 1977; Bartol and Halanchock, 1979; Farrington et al., 1982). Although differences have not been found between criminal and noncriminal populations, differences in the level of extraversion have been found between criminal populations with respect to *types* of crime (Gossop and Kristjansson, 1977; Bartol and Halanchock, 1979).

In sum, Eysenck's theory is a long way from scientific fact. He acknowledges that "the theory here developed is indeed just that... it will need a great deal more empirical evidence to put the theory on more adequate footing..." Eysenck, 1984:99). While overall support for Eysenck's theory is presently weak, it is worth noting an observation made by Bartol and Bartol about Eysenck's theory: they praise it as "one of the few attempts by a psychologist to formulate a general theory of criminal behavior" (Bartol and Bartol, 1986:47).

Wilson and Herrnstein: Reinforcers and Traits

James Q. Wilson, political scientist, and Richard J. Herrnstein, experimental psychologist, have written a book entitled *Crime and Human Nature: The Definitive Study Of The Causes Of Crime* (1985), which combines various theoretical perspectives. Wilson and Herrnstein's theory may be considered an integrated theoretical approach (Siegel, 1989): they themselves refer to the theory as "eclectic, drawing from different, sometimes opposing, schools of thought" (Wilson and Herrnstein, 1985:43). Whatever the classification, Wilson and Herrnstein's theory combines at least two different theoretical orientations, one which entails the use of numerous traits as indicators or predictors of criminal behavior. The other theoretical dimension resembles operant conditioning principles (to be discussed more thoroughly in the next chapter).

At the core of Wilson and Herrnstein's (1985) theory is the assumption that individuals make choices based upon their perceived consequences. They assert: "A person will do that thing the consequences of which are perceived by him or her to be preferable to the consequences of doing something else" (Wilson and Herrnstein, 1985:43). The conception of choice used by Wilson and Herrnstein is not an existential choice, but a choice based upon rewards and losses. "The larger the ratio of the net rewards of crime to the net rewards of noncrime, the greater the tendency to commit the crime" (Wilson and Herrnstein, 1985:44). Rewards from committing crime consist of "material gains... intangible benefits, such as obtaining emotional or sexual gratification, receiving the approval of peers... enhancing one's sense of justice" (Wilson and Herrnstein, 1985:44). Rewards from not choosing crime include avoiding the wrath of such things as guilt, stigma, reputation, and victim retaliation.

Wilson and Herrnstein link trait perspectives to their theory when they assert that "[p]eople who break the law are often psychologically atypical" (1985:173). Wilson and Herrnstein devote almost a quarter of their more than 600 page book to discussing the relationship of particular biological and psychological traits to crime. They assert that "[c]riminals are more likely than noncriminals to have mesomorphic body types... to be somewhat lower in intelligence... to be impulsive or extroverted..."(Wilson and Herrnstein, 1985:66). Some other traits, which according to Wilson and Herrnstein offenders score higher on than nonoffenders, include fearlessness, poor conditionability, aggressiveness, hyperactivity, unconventionality and left-handedness (1985:173-209).

There is no doubt that the traits alluded to above play an important role in Wilson and Herrnstein's general theory, as they argue: "[t]he offender offends not just because of immediate needs and circumstances but also because of enduring personal characteristics, some of whose traces can be found in his [sic] behavior from early childhood..." (1985:209). As for traits being the sole determinant of behavior, they claim that "taken alone they do not constitute a theory of crime, for they do not place the would-be offender in the full context of the reinforcements acting on his behavior" (Wilson and Herrnstein, 1985:66). Taken together, these statements suggest that Wilson and Herrnstein (1985) see crime as a product of "atypical" individual characteristics which, if not controlled through proper conditioning and reinforcement, result in criminal behavior.

Although Wilson and Herrnstein have amassed a large body of research supporting their assumptions of criminal traits, many critics have suggested that the research used is methodologically flawed in many important respects (Siegel, 1989; Gottfredson and Hirschi, 1990). Many of the studies conducted by Wilson and Herrnstein have been criticized for "sampling inadequacy, questionable measurement techniques, and observer bias"

(Siegel, 1989:150). Other criticisms of Wilson and Herrnstein's theory originate in the realm of ethics and constitutional law. For instance, one critic points out the policy implications suggested by Wilson and Herrnstein's theory: "one's constitutional rights will be dependent upon demonstrating specific biological or genetic traits" (Galliher, 1991:247). Overall, critics of Wilson and Herrnstein's theory suggest the need for a meticulous judgment in discriminating between the data presented and underlying interpretations of it.

Gottfredson and Hirschi: The Elements of Self Control

Michael Gottfredson and Travis Hirschi (1990) have proposed a general theory of crime that contains aspects of a trait orientation. Their theory expands classical criminology to encompass a self-control concept (for a traditional explanation of classical criminology see Vold and Bernard, 1986). Gottfredson and Hirschi's version of classical theory suggests that individuals act in order to increase pleasure. Crime is a natural act to enhance pleasure when social control is absent. According to Gottfredson and Hirschi, humans are by nature asocial (1990:86).

Gottfredson and Hirschi espouse the classical view of pleasure-driven individuals, but add to it a refined concept of self-control. They state: "What classical theory lacks is an explicit idea of self-control, the idea that people also differ in the extent to which they are vulnerable to the temptations of the moment" (Gottfredson and Hirschi, 1990:87). Gottfredson and Hirschi go on to argue that individuals who have low self-control tend to be more likely to commit crime. However, a "lack of self-control does not require crime and can be counteracted by situational conditions or other properties of the individual" (Gottfredson and Hirschi, 1990:89). In the same breath, they contend "that high self-control effectively reduces crime..." (Gottfredson and Hirschi, 1990:89). In short, because all individuals strive to enhance pleasure, criminality is much more likely among individuals possessing low levels of self-control than it is among those possessing high levels.

The focus of Gottfredson and Hirschi's general theory, then, is to identify measurable elements of self-control which may aid in identifying those with low self-control. Elements of their self-control construct include individual psychological attributes such as impulsiveness, insensitivity, physicality, risk-taking, short sightedness, and nonverbality (Gottfredson and Hirschi, 1990:90). Gottfredson and Hirschi claim that those lacking self-control tend to measure highly on these attributes. They conclude:

> Since these traits can be identified prior to the age of responsibility for crime, since there is considerable tendency for these traits to come together in the same people, and since the traits tend to persist through life, it seems reasonable to consider them as comprising a stable construct useful in the explanation of crime (Gottfredson and Hirschi, 1990:91).

It is important to stress that for Gottfredson and Hirschi low self control does not automatically imply that individuals will commit crime. Other noncriminal behaviors epitomizing low self-control according to their theory are smoking, drinking, drugs, illicit sex, and gambling (Gottfredson and Hirschi, 1990).

To reiterate, according to Gottfredson and Hirschi, pleasure is a universal drive pursued by all individuals. What prevents some individuals from committing criminal activity is the amount of self-control or conscience they possess. The elements of self-control can be empirically assessed through measuring key psychological traits (i.e., impulsiveness, insensitivity, risk-taking, etc.). Those with low levels of self-control are more likely to commit criminal acts in the name of pleasure. Low self-control is a result of ineffective child-rearing which, according to Gottfredson and Hirschi (1990), occurs when inadequate socialization conditions are present. They suggest three necessary conditions for adequate socialization: "1) monitor the child's behavior; 2) recognize deviant behavior when it occurs; 3) punish such behavior" (1990:97). The other agency they rely on for instilling a strong sense of self control is the school.

Because of the relatively recent emergence of Gottfredson and Hirschi's theory, it has yet to be subjected to rigorous empirical investigation. A study conducted by Keane et al. (1993), however, found a relationship between low self-control and driving under the influence of alcohol, while a study by Grasmick et al. (1993) and a dissertation conducted by Driscoll (1992) found mixed results regarding the validity of the self-control concept. Before judgment can be passed on this particular perspective much more empirical testing is needed.

SUMMARY

Our discussion of trait perspectives in criminal psychology began with those early theorists who believed that criminal behavior was determined by physical and biological constitutions. These early theorists were not psychologists, but physical anthropologists. Their connection, however, with this chapter and criminal psychology in general is twofold. First, their attempt to identify physical attributes that were correlated with criminal behavior paved the way for psychologists to do the same sort of research, using instead behavioral characteristics. Second, the analytical dissection of humans into classification schemes has provided the epistemological focus of all criminal trait orientations as physiological, biological, psychological or a combination thereof.

Next, we discussed briefly the use of IQ testing and personality inventories in explaining criminal behavior. With little surprise, the data regarding these eclectic approaches remains inconclusive. In addition, such eclectic approaches to identifying criminal traits run the risk of discriminating through reification of the ideas and values of the dominant culture and producing circular explanations of causation.

In the last section of this chapter we focused on contemporary theoretical trait perspectives. All of these contemporary trait perspectives were much more complex than their early counterparts discussed at the beginning of this chapter. They combined different disciplinary and theoretical perspectives to formulate general theoretical explanations of criminal behavior. Although none of these theories have been shown to be highly predictive of criminal behavior, they do, nevertheless, provide us with some conceptual explanations of the complexity of human behavior.

Four

Behavioral, Situational and Social Learning Perspectives

ONE OF THE most popular explanations of criminal behavior from both psychological and sociological disciplines is that it is learned. Psychologists have generally dealt with the individual process of learning criminal behavior, whereas sociologists have dealt with the group and structural context of learning. This chapter explores the modification of learning theory as developed in psychology and in the study of crime.

Like modern trait perspectives, learning perspectives also developed in opposition to the psychoanalytical perspective. Learning theorists' aversion to psychoanalysis is grounded in a skepticism about the forces of the unconscious mind in determining behavior and the subjective nature of the psychoanalytical approach to personality. Given this, early learning theorists set out to formulate a theory of behavior grounded in observable facts. Early learning theorists believed that behavior which could not be observed was not a worthy subject of inquiry.

Unlike trait approaches, learning theories do not assume that people are born with fixed repertoires of behaviors. Learning theorists simply assume that behavior is learned; they attempt to explain the process of how certain behaviors are acquired. Although they do acknowledge biological predispositions as factors which influence an individual's ability to learn, they remain committed to the belief that all behavior, good or bad, is learned. Criminal behavior is acquired; it is not the product of a biological or psychological trait.

Learning theories in psychology can be separated into three main schools: classical conditioning, operant or instrumental conditioning, and social learning. Each school has in some way been used in the study of crime to explain behavior, either in conjunction with another theoretical perspective or by itself. This chapter focuses upon the development of each school and the contribution it has made to the study of crime.

CLASSICAL CONDITIONING AND CRIME

Classical conditioning is historically the oldest learning perspective, and the weakest with respect to providing an all-encompassing explanation of the complexity of human behavior. Because it assumes that its subjects, humans and animals, are extremely passive, it is the weakest explanation of our ability to learn. In classical conditioning the subject learns by association; other behavioral factors like motivation, rewards, or environmental manipulation are not accounted for in the conditioning process. Many of our simple behaviors, however, can be accounted for through classical conditioning. As we shall see, Hans Eysenck (1984) combines his trait perspective with classical conditioning to account for why some individuals with the same biological makeup commit crimes while others do not.

A Russian, Ivan Petrovich Pavlov (1849-1936), was the first to discover the concept of classical conditioning while doing experiments on dogs (Massey, 1981). Pavlov, a Nobel Prize winner, has been described by some as more of a physiologist than a psychologist (see for example, Miller, 1962; Samuel, 1981). Nevertheless, Pavlov's discovery of classical conditioning laid yet another foundation for a scientific approach to the study of behavior which eventually led to more sophisticated learning theories.

Pavlov discovered classical conditioning while conducting experiments on dogs' salivation and digestion. Pavlov created an experimental setting in which a dog was placed in a harness and forced to look forward in one direction at a window. Just below the dog's head was a pan in which meat powder was poured. Pavlov found that a dog could be conditioned to salivate at the sight of a light or the sound of a tone (condition stimulus) by learning that it signaled food. In other words, a dog could be conditioned to associate a light or particular tone with food. Pavlov was successful with both lights and tones in conditioning the dogs' behavior (Atkinson et al., 1981).

Conditioning is accomplished by turning on a light, waiting a few seconds, then delivering some meat powder into the dog's dish; consequently, the dog begins to salivate profusely. Initially, the sight of the light does not cause the dog to salivate. Through many trials, however, the dog eventually begins to salivate at the first glimpse of the light. The classical conditioning process is complete when the light is turned on and the dog salivates copiously without any meat powder being delivered into the dish. The dog has at this point learned to associate the light with food. This is what Pavlov means by a conditioned response or what psychologists have come to call classical conditioning.

Unconditioned responses (UC) are those behaviors which are not learned, but are in essence natural to an organism. In this particular example, the dog salivating when it smells the meat is an unconditioned response, because smelling meat and salivating is a natural and not a learned function. The meat is called an unconditioned stimulus (US). In the example given above, the light represents a conditioned stimulus (CS). That is, a dog normally does not salivate at the sight of a light, but when it learns to associate the light with food its behavior has been conditioned. The CS (i.e., light) causes the dog to expect food, which creates a conditioned response, salivation (Atkinson et al., 1981:194-197).

One of the most radical proponents of Pavlovian classical conditioning was John B. Watson (1879-1958). Watson received the first Ph.D. in psychology from the University of Chicago and is noted for being the first to think of psychology as a scientific study of behavior (Massey, 1981; Samuel, 1981). In a famous paper, Watson (1913) founded the school of "behaviorism." He believed that concepts like consciousness, mind, will, and so on are not meaningful variables in the study of behavior. Behavior should be studied using as data only observations of stimuli and responses (Samuel, 1981). By adhering to the canons of positive science, Watson believed that human behavior could be predicted and controlled. Watson went so far as to assert that distinctions between humans and other animals are irrelevant to the learning process (Massey, 1981).

Watson's significance to the learning perspective stems from his application of classical conditioning principles to the behavioral study of humans, specifically infants and children. Watson (1924:76) once remarked:

> Give me a dozen healthy infants, well-formed, and my own specified world to bring them up in and I'll guarantee to take any one at random and train him to become any type of specialist I might select — doctor, lawyer, artist, merchant-chief and yes, even into beggar-man and thief, regardless of his [sic] talents, penchants, tendencies, abilities, vocations, and race of his ancestors.

Many of Watson's experiments on infants and children would probably never pass a university ethics board today. Nevertheless, Watson believed, as his statement above makes clear, that humans can be conditioned to perform whatever behavior is expected. Watson's application of classical conditioning to human learning paved the way for Hans Eysenck's use of classical conditioning to account for why some people with the same biological traits commit crime while others do not.

Eysenck's Version of Classical Conditioning and Crime

As noted in Chapter Three, Eysenck's personality theory fuses a trait perspective with a classical learning perspective to formulate an integrated theory. As elaborated in Chapter Three, Eysenck's theory is based on the assumption that a biological predisposition frames the psychological constitution of the individual. The other dimension of Eysenck's theory is the use of classical conditioning to explain how an individual learns the rules and laws that govern society. The content and intensity of conditioning is what determines whether an individual will become law-abiding or antisocial.

For Eysenck, antisocial behavior "is a natural type of behavior for all animals and infants" (1984:92). This assumption is similar to the Freudian concept of the id and the Hobbesian belief that individuals are hedonistic or pleasure seeking. Eysenck goes on to claim that "[s]ocialized behavior, which often goes against the interest of the individual, although it is in line with the best interest of society, does require an explanation; it is, in a very real sense, 'unnatural'!" (1984:92). From this premise, Eysenck believes that punishments for norm violations, administered by parents, school authorities and even peers, act as unconditioned stimuli.

In order to place Eysenck's conditioning perspective of socialization in the Pavlovian classical conditioning model, one must remember that a child is asocial by nature and is made social by conditioning. In Pavlov's experiment, the unconditioned response consists of the dog's salivation in natural response to the meat powder. The meat powder is an unconditioned stimulus because it naturally produces salivation. Just as meat produces saliva in dogs, socializing authorities, according to Eysenck, produce fear, pain, or anxiety in infants and children. The unconditioned response, then, is the child's fear, pain or anxiety with the unconditioned stimuli being parents, school authorities, or peers. The conditioned response in Pavlov's experiment was the dog's salivation at the sight of the light; the conditioned stimulus being the light. For Eysenck, the child's conditioned response is the inclination toward social behavior. That is, through numerous trials, the child begins to associate pain, fear or anxiety with the conditioned stimulus, the thought or act of committing an antisocial behavior.

The biological or trait factor of Eysenck's theory contends that some individuals will need more social conditioning than others, because of their predisposition (e.g., extraverts). The social conditioning dimension focuses exclusively on "the content of the socialization process" (Eysenck, 1984:93). The individual's conscience, then, is a product of intense social conditioning. In a sense, conscience becomes for Eysenck a "conditioned reflex" (Bartol and Bartol, 1986:42).

According to Eysenck, any individual regardless of biological predisposition can be conditioned to be a law-abiding citizen (1984). Ostensibly, Eysenck's solution to antisocial behavior is to increase the intensity of the social conditioning process. He states:

> there has been an increase in permissiveness which has preceded and accompanied the increase in crime, and in our hypothesis it is precisely the lack of conditioning contingencies produced by the permissive atmosphere in home, school, and court which would produce such a lessening of the 'conscience' or moral fibre of the population (Eysenck, 1984:99).

Although Eysenck's theoretical approach to the cause of crime is unique, his solution to the problem of crime is a common one. He basically advocates tightening disciplinary controls in the major socializing agencies like the family, school, and legal agencies (For an assessment of the evidence supporting Eysenck's theory see Chapter Three).

Eysenck's personality theory is the only psychological theory of criminal behavior that uses the classical conditioning aspect of learning exclusively. Undeniably, the classical conditioning aspect of learning is important, but strict reliance on it to explain all criminal behavior is facile. Bartol and Bartol note that Eysenck's reliance on "classical conditioning as a primary explanation of criminality and his tendency to ignore other forms of learning and mediational (cognitive) processes may be the theory's most damaging weakness" (1986:47). With this criticism in mind, we shall move on to the next modification in learning theory.

OPERANT CONDITIONING AND CRIME

Before embarking on a discussion of the applications of operant conditioning principles to the study of crime, it is necessary to distinguish operant from classical conditioning and to explain its origins. The key element distinguishing classical conditioning from operant conditioning is that classical conditioning involves association of two things and operant conditioning involves linking causally the response to a stimulus and its consequence. In classical conditioning the dog learned to associate the light with the meat powder, salivating whenever it saw the light. The dog salivating to the meat is a normal and passive response. Operant conditioning, on the other hand, is active: it requires that an agent act in a reflexive way on the environment, which then brings about a consequence. For further clarification of the operant conditioning perspective let us turn to its major advocate.

The main proponent and innovator of operant conditioning and behaviorism is Burrhus Frederick Skinner (1904-1991). Skinner began his academic career as an English major at Hamilton College with the goal of becoming a writer. When this aspiration did not pan out, Skinner went to graduate school at Harvard where he received his Ph.D. in psychology in 1931 (Massey, 1981). Some have suggested that Skinner may be the most prominent American psychologist of the 20th century (Bartol and Bartol, 1986:79). Skinner's operant principles have been used to theorize about criminal behavior and have been applied in institutional settings such as schools, mental health facilities, and correctional sites (Bartol and Bartol,

1986; Massey, 1981).

Skinner (1980) did not acknowledge a human nature that portrayed humans one way or another; that is, he did not perceive human beings as having a predisposition towards being good or bad. Although Skinner did acknowledge that individuals have different genetic endowments, he perceived this as of little concern. Skinner's assumptions about humans differs immensely from a psychoanalytical perspective, which contends that humans confront the world with an asocial disposition driven by instincts; it also differs from a trait orientation which contends that behavior is determined by a physiological, biological or psychological predisposition. For Skinner (1980) and behaviorists in general, good and bad behaviors are relative determinations designated and sanctioned by human societies. Whether an individual's behavior is good or bad depends upon the reinforcing environment which either rewards or punishes particular behaviors. Given this assumption, criminal behavior is learned through reinforcement.

Skinner, like Watson, was a radical behaviorist who believed that the purpose of psychology was also to predict and control human behavior. In fact, many of Skinner's books specifically address the themes of prediction and control. For instance, in a novel titled *Walden Two* (1948), Skinner creates an utopian society based on a reinforcement schedule specific to each individual's needs. In another book by Skinner, *Science and Human Behavior* (1953), he portrays how social institutions (e.g., government, law, education, etc.,) control behavior through operant conditioning.

Probably the most controversial book written by Skinner is *Beyond Freedom and Dignity* (1980 [1971]) wherein Skinner argues in favor of designing societies on the basis of operant conditioning principles. Altering "bad" behavior would be accomplished through redesigning the environment so that it does not reinforce "bad" behavior. In this book, Skinner clearly outlines a scientific conception of humankind in which all aspects of behavior can be predicted and controlled based upon the reinforcement contingencies of the environment.

To highlight the extent to which Skinner believed that humans were subject to control, we have included a passage from the last chapter of *Beyond Freedom and Dignity*:

> An experimental analysis shifts the determination of behavior from autonomous man [sic] to the environment—an environment

> responsible both for the evolution of the species and for the repertoire acquired by each member... Is man then "abolished"? Certainly not as a species or as an individual achiever. It is the autonomous inner man who is abolished, and that is a step forward. But does man not then become merely a victim or passive observer of what is happening to him? He is indeed controlled by his environment, but we must remember that it is an environment largely of his own making. The evolution of a culture is a gigantic exercise in self-control... We have not yet seen what man can make of man (Skinner, 1980:205-206).

For Skinner, free will and self-determination are illusionary concepts that have no place in the scientific study of behavior. The environment, as he notes, is the controlling source of human behavior; it is by manipulating the environment that human behavior can be predicted and controlled.

The elaboration of operant conditioning is Skinner's contribution to learning theory. Operant means that an organism acts on the environment. In classical conditioning, (which Skinner espoused initially, but thought inadequate to account for all learning), an organism simply reacts to some sort of stimulus like Pavlov's dog. Skinner referred to classical conditioning as respondent behavior— organisms reacting directly to a stimulus. Operant conditioning, on the other hand, involves the organism acting on the environment to produce consequences. The type of consequence, either pleasant or unpleasant, determines whether or not the particular behavior will be repeated. In short, consequences are either reinforced (encouraged) or punished (discouraged).

To illustrate Skinner's operant principles it may be helpful to refer to his rat experiments. Skinner designed an apparatus for operant conditioning which is now referred to as the Skinner box. Inside a Skinner box there is an extended bar with a food container underneath it. A rat is placed in the box to explore the limited surroundings. Eventually the rat begins to press the bar in the box. Each time it does, a food pellet is dropped into its dish. The rat learns that by pressing the bar (i.e., acting on the environment) it receives food, an active behavior reinforced with a pleasant consequence.

The chief means by which operant conditioning increases the probability of a predicted outcome is through the establishment of a reinforcement schedule. Using our example above, a reinforcement schedule would be a rat pressing the bar five times in order to receive one food pellet. This is called a ratio schedule. A reinforcement schedule based on a reinforcement every two minutes is called an interval schedule. And a reinforcement schedule which is not based on a ratio or a time sequence is referred to as a variable interval schedule. The variable interval schedule (also referred to as an intermittent schedule) is probably most representative of the kind of reinforcement we experience in our daily lives (Massey, 1981).

Operant conditioning involves two different types of reinforcers. A primary reinforcer is a basic need like food or water. A secondary reinforcer, could be money, because money is not a physical necessity, but can be used to satisfy many different needs.

Reinforcers are also divided into the categories of positive and negative. When we are positively reinforced, it means we get some sort of pleasure or satisfaction as a consequence of performing a particular behavior: we get a reward. For instance, studying hard in school usually leads to academic accolades and parental lauding— both positive, secondary reinforcements. Negative reinforcement occurs when an unpleasant experience or sensation is discontinued as the consequence of a particular behavior. For instance, if a professor wishes her students to keep up with their reading assignments, she may use a series of weekly quizzes as insurance. Once the students have acquired the desired habit of getting the reading done on time, the professor may stop giving the quizzes. As a consequence of the behavior (reading on time) the students have been freed from an unpleasant condition (the quiz). Punishment means to suffer pain or discomfort as the consequence of behavior. Punishment is used only to discourage, while both positive and negative reinforcement are intended to encourage behaviors. Skinner saw punishment as being an ineffective way to change a behavior (Bartol and Bartol, 1986).

Criticisms of Skinner's behaviorism focus on his refusal to deal with any human attributes or dimensions that lie outside the realm of observation. Skinner denies any notion of an individual ego or self, and basically treats humans as empty containers (Samuel, 1981). Carl Rogers (1963) has also criticized Skinner for his contradiction regarding his own personal ego and his theoretical treatment of humans as empty containers. A more controversial aspect of Skinner's behaviorism is the belief that human behavior is totally predictable (Samuel, 1981). As of now, the prediction of human behavior has been quite unsuccessful.

Other damaging criticisms target the limitations in Skinner's operant principles in accounting for all human behavior (Bartol and Bartol, 1986).

One of the chief critics of using operant principles to account for all human behavior is Albert Bandura (1973, 1977, 1983). A discussion of Bandura's work will follow shortly.

With this as a general overview of operant conditioning principles, we will now turn our attention towards some of the theorists applying operant conditioning principles to an explanation of crime causation. We begin our discussion with C.R. Jeffery.

C.R. Jeffery's Operant Conditioning Perspective on Crime

Jeffery's "Theory of Differential Reinforcement" is an attempt to revise and empirically verify Edwin Sutherland's theory of "differential association." As Jeffery states, "[t]he purpose of this paper is to apply modern learning theory to differential association in order to place it in modern dress and to place it in a form which is empirically testable" (1965:294). Despite Jeffery's intentions, we make the argument later on that Sutherland's learning theory is a highly complex approach to the explanation of crime hence, the attempt to reduce it to operant principles greatly alters the scope and meaning embodied in Sutherland's perspective. Nevertheless, Jeffery's theory is the first attempt to use operant principles as an explanation for crime causation (Nietzel, 1979; Bartol, 1986).

Jeffery treats criminal behavior as operant behavior by suggesting that its perpetuation is due to the "changes it produces on the environment" (1965:295). Stealing, for example, produces a desired item (e.g., a car, bike, stereo, etc.), which acts as positive reinforcement for the criminal act. For Jeffery, the existence of a legal system designed to punish offenders is not always enough to deter a potential offender, especially when an offender has been reinforced for past crimes. Jeffery asserts, "a criminal act occurs in an environment in which in the past the actor has been reinforced for behaving in this manner, and the aversive consequences attached to the behavior have been of such a nature that they do not control or prevent the response" (1965:295). Punishment may not be enough to prevent an individual from committing a crime, because the reinforcement of past criminal behavior overrides the threat of punishment.

According to Jeffery, the source of criminal behavior can be found in the consequences of the behavior. Stealing an automobile either entails a potential reward or a severe punishment. If an individual is aware of both consequences, then what determines her/his choice? In order to address this question, Jeffery (1965:295-296) makes these assumptions:

1. The reinforcing quality of different stimuli differ for different actors depending on the past conditioning of each;

2. some individuals have been reinforced for criminal behavior whereas other individuals have not been;

3. some individuals have been punished for criminal behavior whereas others have not been; and

4. an individual will be intermittently reinforced and/or punished for criminal behavior, that is, he will not be reinforced or punished every time he commits a criminal act.

Ultimately the maintenance of criminal behavior, for Jeffery, is the excess of reinforcement over punishment for a particular behavior.

In addition to providing an explanation of crime, Jeffery's theory of differential reinforcement also accounts for why some individuals living in similar situations may commit crimes while the others do not. This is an attempt to do away with broader sociological generalizations that contend crime is a product of learned associations in a particular milieu. Jeffery gives an example in which he notes three variables that point to why individuals differ in their behavior regarding theft, even though they are products of the same environment: "1) the reinforcing quality of the stolen item; 2) past stealing responses which have been reinforced, and 3) past stealing responses which have been punished (1965:296). Thus, if two brothers grow up in an economically deprived environment and one becomes a thief and the other a minister, the reason for the discrepancy is because each one had a different conditioning history. The brother who became a minister associated theft with punishment more than reward. For the brother who became a thief, the associations were reversed.

Jeffery also discusses how negative reinforcement can be used to account for criminal behavior. He offers an example of a situation where a husband kills his wife for infidelity. The consequence of killing the wife alleviates a painful emotional situation caused by the wife's infidelity. Hence, the act of murder in this situation leads to negative reinforcement

(Jeffery, 1965:296).

According to operant conditioning principles, punishment means the removal of a reinforcement or the creation of an aversive stimulus to discourage a behavior. Like Skinner's theory, Jeffery's theory of differential reinforcement contends that relentless or severe punishment will not eradicate an undesirable behavior. Jeffery suggests, however, that punishment can be effective if it is immediate and consistent in its application. For example, if punishment were to be administered very shortly after a crime was committed, Jeffery argues, the effect upon behavior would be more pronounced.

Jeffery notes that the current structure of the legal system is not designed to punish with certainty, which creates in the criminals behavior an "avoidance response." This simply means that individuals will avoid the aversive consequences of criminal acts by using some of the following techniques: "avoid detection, don't leave fingerprints, hire a good lawyer, bribe the police, plead guilty to a reduced charge, plead insanity..." Jeffery, 1965:299). Jeffery goes on to argue that "[l]aw enforcement procedures shape a great deal of avoidance and escape behavior, but this can be quite unrelated to the behavior that the law is trying to prevent and control" (1965:299). This point may be true on some counts, but Jeffery offers no solution to the current legal structure, nor does he deal with the implications of altering the concepts of procedural law to produce celerity in punishment.

With this as an overview of Jeffery's theory of differential reinforcement, we will now move on to a similar approach using operant principles proposed by Robert Burgess and Ronald Akers (1966). Due to the similarity of these two approaches we will reserve critical commentary of the operant approach to crime for the end of the section.

Burgess and Akers: Differential Association-Reinforcement

Like Jeffery's differential reinforcement, Burgess and Akers' (1966) theory of "Differential Association-Reinforcement" is an attempt to provide more concrete operational definitions and empirical referents to Sutherland's theory of "Differential Association." Burgess and Akers state: "We are basically in agreement with Jeffery that learning theory has progressed to the point where it seems likely that differential association can be rested in a more sophisticated and testable form in the language of modern learning theory" (1966:131). Although in agreement with the basic purpose of Jeffery's attempt to revise Sutherland's theory, Burgess and Akers (1966) contend that his theoretical effort falls short on two accounts. The first shortcoming, according to Burgess and Akers (1966), is that Jeffery fails to provide an adequate link between operant learning principles and Sutherland's theory. Their second criticism of Jeffery deals with his reliance on experimental data dealing with animals rather than humans (Burgess and Akers, 1966).

Burgess and Akers (1966) attempt to rectify these perceived shortcomings in Jeffery's reiteration of Sutherland's theory. In order to accomplish this task, they reformulate the propositions in Sutherland's theory of "differential association" to conform to operant conditioning principles. Burgess and Akers' (1966) claim that they are modernizing Sutherland's theory. In their modernization attempt, however, we believe that they are in essence changing the context and focus of Sutherland's learning theory, and in so doing have created their own operant theory of crime. Thus we treat Burgess and Akers' (1966) reformulation of Sutherland's propositions as their own operant theory about crime and reserve our discussion of Sutherland's original propositions for the next section in this chapter.

Burgess and Akers' (1966) "differential association-reinforcement theory of criminal behavior" is an operant conditioning theory. It holds as its basic premise the belief that criminal behavior is generated and maintained by operant reinforcement. As such, all behavior according to Burgess and Akers can be empirically accounted for without making reference to any sort of individual a priori needs or motivations. They believe "that 'needs' are unobservable, hypothetical, fictional inner-causal agents which were usually invented on the spot to provide spurious explanations of some observable behavior" (Burgess and Akers, 1966:144). With this in mind, the first proposition of Burgess and Akers' theory reads as follows: "**I) Criminal behavior is learned according to the principles of operant conditioning**" (1966:137). Burgess and Akers (1966) identify six environmental consequences that reinforce or shape behavior based on operant principles.

The first and second types of environmental consequence, which have been noted above, are positive and negative reinforcement. Positive reinforcement is a stimulus which when applied increases the frequency of a behavior. Negative reinforcement is a stimulus which increases the frequency of a behavior when withdrawn.

Aversive stimuli, or punishers, are a third type of environmental consequence. These stimuli (e.g., spanking or verbal reprimands) decrease the frequency of a behavior because their application is unpleasant. The fourth type of environmental consequence is negative punishment. Negative punishment occurs when a particular behavior eliminates a certain pleasurable stimulus (e.g., a child's allowance or desert), which causes the behavior to decrease in frequency. The stimuli eliminated in this case are considered positive reinforcers (Burgess and Akers, 1966). For example, a child may get attention for throwing a tantrum or may be ignored entirely; if the child is ignored, then her/his behavior may be eliminated— hence negative punishment.

Stimuli which neither increase or decrease certain behavior are called neutral stimuli. This is the fifth possible consequence that a behavior may have on an environment. The sixth type of a consequence a behavior may have on a particular environment is that it no longer produces a stimulus event. "The stimuli which are produced are neutral stimuli and the process extinction" (Burgess and Akers, 1966:133). A behavior simply has no effect on an environment in which it takes place and thus ceases to exist.

With these six environmental consequences providing the basis for how behavior is learned, Burgess and Akers go on to formulate a second proposition which deals with details of the situational learning environment. Their second proposition reads: "II) **Criminal behavior is learned both in nonsocial situations that are reinforcing or discriminative, and through the social interaction in which the behavior of other persons is reinforcing or discriminative for criminal behavior**" (Burgess and Akers, 1966:139). In this proposition, Burgess and Akers (1966) provide a framework which accounts for how criminal behavior may be learned in settings that do not provide social reinforcement or interaction with others. That is, because most criminal behaviors are self-reinforcing, behaviors may be learned without any interaction or verbal contact with another individual (Burgess and Akers, 1966). This proposition also claims that individuals discriminate between situations and persons based upon their reinforcement value. Accordingly, children may obey their parents when the parents are present, but in the midst of their peers they may engage in deviant behavior because of its reinforcement value.

Their third proposition professes: "**III) The principal part of the learning of criminal behavior occurs in those groups which comprise the individual's major source of reinforcement**" (Burgess and Akers, 1966:140). Burgess and Akers (1966) suggest that the family usually does the majority of social training and provides the most influential system of reinforcers. As the child grows older, however, peer groups may become the major reinforcer of behavior. The ultimate cause of criminal behavior here points once again to the early influences of the family.

Proposition four maintains: "**IV) The learning of criminal behavior, including specific techniques, attitudes, and avoidance procedures, is a function of the effective and available reinforcers, and the existing reinforcement contingencies**" (Burgess and Akers, 1966:141). Burgess and Akers assert that "the nature of the reinforcer system and the reinforcement contingencies are crucial determinants of individual and group behavior" (1966:141). As such, a knowledge of the situational factors as well as the system of social and nonsocial reinforcers would enable the theorist to unveil the determinants of a particular behavior. This proposition rests on the assumption that the information necessary for predicting behavioral outcomes based on operant principles could be clearly established into operationalized dependent and independent variables.

The fifth proposition put forth by Burgess and Akers contends that: "**V) The specific class of behaviors which are learned and their frequency of occurrence are a function of the reinforcers which are effective and available, and the rules or norms by which these reinforcers are applied**" (1966:142). This proposition attempts to account for how specific norms and values are incorporated into behavior through the various types of reinforcers. In this vein, criminal behavior becomes a matter of definition, whereby one group defines the norms and values of another group as criminal or deviant (Burgess and Akers, 1966:142).

The sixth proposition which follows from the fifth states:"**VI) Criminal behavior is a function of norms which are discriminative for criminal behavior, the learning of which takes place when such behavior is more reinforced than noncriminal behavior.**" (Burgess and Akers, 1966:143-144). This proposition is based on the assumption that a dominant behavior results because it has been the most reinforced either positively or negatively. Thus, criminal behavior occurs "under those conditions where an individual has been most highly reinforced for such behavior, and the aversive consequences contingent upon the behavior have been of such a nature that they do not perform a 'punishment function'" (Burgess and Akers, 1966:143).

The final proposition of Burgess and Akers' theory declares that:"**VII) The strength of criminal behavior is a direct function of the amount, frequency and probability of its reinforcement**" (1966:144). According to this contention criminal behavior is a result of a conditioning history favoring reinforcement conducive to the preservation of criminal behavior. Of course, the proof of this proposition rests on the assumption that a quantitative assessment of the reinforcement schedule of any particular behavior can be made.

Burgess and Akers' (1966) have attempted to provide a theory which they claim has all testable propositions. The picture they paint of human beings is somewhat complex but mechanical. They believe that if provided with an adequate amount of information, using operant principles, causality can be shown to successfully predict behavior. In sum, their theory provides an explanation of how delinquent behavior starts and how it is sustained.

Akers (1977, 1985) has gone on to refine aspects of this theory by incorporating the modeling aspect of learning posited in Bandura's social learning theory and acknowledgement of self reinforcement (yet to be discussed). For the most part, however, his theory retains the basic Skinnerian premise that behavior is learned and maintained by external factors. As Bartol and Bartol suggest "[a]lthough Akers recognizes self-reinforcement, he treats it as a social reinforcer, suggesting that when people reinforce themselves, they are really acting in the role of others, as if these others were present" (1986:90). They go on to point out that "[t]he fact that we can reward or punish ourselves personally, independent of societal expectations, is apparently not relevant to Akers" (Bartol and Bartol, 1986:90). Note, the key differentiating factor between operant principles and social learning theory is the concept of self-motivation and reinforcement. This distinction will be made clear shortly.

There is yet one more theory that needs a brief note because it fits within the operant perspective. After completing this, we will examine criticisms of the operant view of human behavior and crime. For now, let us return to Wilson and Herrnstein (1985) for their version of how operant conditioning principles influence criminal behavior.

Wilson and Herrnstein: A Theory of Reinforcers

As noted in Chapter Three, Wilson and Herrnstein's (1985) theory of crime combines traits, choice, and classical and operant principles into a general theory of crime. They argue that humans have biological and psychological predispositions which, in conjunction with classical and operant conditioning, greatly influence how individuals make choices. We have already noted in Chapter Three some of the trait predispositions that they suggest are associated with a certain propensity toward criminal behavior. However, as we also noted in Chapter Three, Wilson and Herrnstein (1985) do not see trait predispositions as the sole cause of criminal behavior. They also see criminal behavior ultimately as a product of choices made by an individual based on the perceived consequences.

Combining both operant and classical conditioning Wilson and Herrnstein assert: "A person will do that thing the consequences of which are perceived by him or her to be preferable to the consequences of doing something else" (1985:43). Choice as Wilson and Herrnstein view it is not an existential choice, but a choice based on rewards and losses. "The larger the ratio of the net rewards of crime to the net rewards of noncrime, the greater the tendency to commit the crime" (Wilson and Herrnstein, 1985:44). Rewards for committing crime consist of "material gains... intangible benefits, such as obtaining emotional or sexual gratification, receiving the approval of peers... enhancing one's sense of justice" (Wilson and Herrnstein, 1985:44). Rewards for not choosing crime include avoiding such things as guilt, stigma, reputation, and victim retaliation.

Important to the individual's decision making is the certainty of punishment from both an operant and classical conditioning perspective. Because in most cases the rewards of crime are experienced prior to their costs, Wilson and Herrnstein (1985) believe that punishment must be certain in order to make the reward of noncrime more appealing. For Wilson and Herrnstein (1985), however, rewards for committing a crime always remain to some degree uncertain. They believe that the way individuals construct conceptually the possibilities of the future largely determines how they make choices. Using operant principles they suggest that "if the threat of being punished oneself is reduced, the rewards for noncrime... are weakened, making noncrime seem less profitable" (Wilson and Herrnstein, 1985:50). The effectiveness of operant conditioning principles according to Wilson and Herrnstein (1985) are most effective with people who can anticipate future consequences.

With respect to classical conditioning principles providing effective restraints on behavior, certainty in punishment is also required. Wilson and Herrnstein offer this account of the effect of classical conditioning on behavior: they profess, "[t]he tendency for the punishment of others to affect the extent to which we feel guilty when we contemplate committing the same crime is an example of the use of classical conditioning" (Wilson and Herrnstein, 1985:50). Even though Wilson and Herrnstein rely on classical and operant principles to account for restraints on behavior, their theory is not true to either approach with respect to the importance of the environment. Wilson and Herrnstein assume that each individual has a particular measurable trait predisposition which affects their ability to be conditioned. This aspect of their theory is unlike traditional operant theory which relies on the environment the most important determinant of behavior. Their use of learning theory can be summed up with these words: "the larger the ratio of the rewards (material and nonmaterial) of noncrime to the rewards (material and nonmaterial) of crime, the weaker the tendency to commit crimes" (1985:61). The scope and forethought involved in appraising the rewards of any one choice is for Wilson and Herrnstein (1985) bound up with a plethora of individual psychological and biological factors. The predisposition of an individual appears to play a larger role in the conditionability of an individual than the reinforcing environment. This is a key differentiating factor which distinguishes their approach from traditional operant theory.

Evaluation Of Operant Perspectives On Crime

Using operant conditioning as the sole explanation for criminal behavior may be too simplistic (Bartol and Bartol, 1986). Also, many have noted that the Skinnerian model is too restricting in accounting for the vast complexity involved in human learning (Bandura, 1983, 1986; Bartol and Bartol, 1986; Clinard, 1974). None of these criticisms, however, suggest that individuals do not learn through classical and operant conditioning. Rather, they suggest that to collapse all types of learned behavior into the rigidity of classical and operant laws is a dangerous oversimplification of human behavior (Bartol and Bartol, 1986).

For one thing, most of the research done on Skinnerian behaviorism is conducted on animals and then inferred to human beings. No doubt this research has established important concepts of learning applicable to human beings; however, as for providing a plenary explanation for all criminal behavior and being a panacea for modifying antisocial behavior in the long term, operant conditioning has proven highly fallible. On the other hand, human beings can be conditioned using classical and operant principles. It is exactly the latter fact that made operant conditioning such an attractive model for criminal justice administrators and clinicians (Bartol and Bartol, 1986).

Believing that antisocial behavior results from a person's reinforcing environment produces a simple rehabilitative solution for criminal justice agents. This solution is to change the environment which reinforces antisocial behavior and recondition the individual to adhere to the prevailing norms of society. As opposed to the long and drawn out nature of psychoanalysis, operant conditioning provides a simple and quick way to eradicate an undesirable behavior (Clinard, 1974). An added incentive to using operant conditioning is that in many cases it works (Bartol and Bartol, 1986).

Many operant conditioning solutions, however, do not deal with the internal dimensions of human behavior, and therefore they may overlook important ethical and humanitarian restraints in their aim to modify behavior to the requirement of society. A good example of this is offered by Clinard (1974) who notes the book and movie *A Clockwork Orange*. The main character in the book is a gang member who commits numerous violent crimes ranging from rape to serious assault. Eventually, this depraved character is apprehended and put into prison where he undergoes aspects of both a classical and operant conditioning program designed to eradicate his violent impulses. The program is a success, but the movie leaves us pondering whether "the ends of social conformity justify the means..." (Clinard, 1974:224). The movie also leads us to question the violence of society in general because once the protagonist has been rendered docile, ironically, he becomes a victim.

A problem endemic to operant conditioning is that its success in a total institution (e.g., prison) may not carry over into the outside world where the environment is much more permeable and in many ways complicated (Clinard, 1974). Consequently, to accommodate the conditioning received in a prison or correctional-type setting, much of the social and physical environment (e.g., areas conducive to crime) would have to be restructured.

When the issue is put in these terms, to most policy makers operant conditioning is less appealing.

Probably the most damning aspect of operant conditioning, however, is its superficial account of human behavior and learning. Bandura notes, "[b]ecause errors can produce costly, or even fatal outcomes, the prospects of survival would be slim indeed if the only way we could learn is by the consequences of our actions" (1986:202). Advocates of operant conditioning have asked us to relegate those internal dimensions of the human mind like thinking, memory, and perception to the realm of meaninglessness. Bartol and Bartol have noted that operant proponents have lost sight of the individual by overemphasizing "the environmental or external determinants of behavior...", thus "overlooking a critical level of explanation" (1986:83). They go on to suggest that we must "[r]emember that human beings are, in part, active problem solvers who perceive, encode, interpret, and make decisions on the basis of what the environment has to offer (Bartol and Bartol, 1986:83). Precisely because classical and operant conditioning do not account for these more complex processes (i.e., thinking and remembering), which indeed influence behavior, they remain incomplete explanations of criminal behavior. In short, classical and operant conditioning do not provide an explanation for "what transpires between the time the organism perceives a stimulus and the time it responds or reacts" (Bartol and Bartol, 1986:83). Classical and operant conditioning do not allow for thinking, introspection, and reflection. We now turn our attention toward a discussion of the more complex dimensions of human learning.

SOCIAL LEARNING THEORIES

A synopsis of social learning theory would suggest that learning is ultimately a product of listening to people and observing them in our social environments (Bartol and Bartol, 1986). Social learning theorists acknowledge the significance of classical and operant conditioning in accounting for many behaviors, but they go beyond this by acknowledging that humans can form hypotheses about future consequences. According to social learning theorists, humans are able to create scenarios of future events and in so doing draw probable conclusions about the consequences of acting in particular ways. Simply put, humans can "'teach' themselves patterns of behavior they have not yet overtly performed. This means that they are able to make plans and achieve insightful solutions to problems" (Samuel, 1981:118).

The difference between the social learning perspective and the behavior producing consequences of operant conditioning is best illustrated with an example. Assume that a young boy observes his older sister selling cocaine on a street corner. His sister has been selling cocaine for a couple of years and is making a lot of money, which enables her to buy nice things for herself. Having observed this behavior, the boy begins to imagine himself selling cocaine and reaping the monetary and materialistic rewards like new clothes, a stereo, car, etc. Based upon the boy's observations and imaginary imitations, he learns to sell the cocaine, and consequently, he reaps the monetary benefits he saw his sister get, and the ones he imagined himself having. The boy's learned behavior continues because it is reinforced by the monetary benefits and by not being caught.

The boy has learned the trade of selling cocaine by observation, not by trial and error. Through the process of imitation and imagination, the boy was able to see himself performing this behavior. In so doing, he provided self reinforcement without having actually acted on the physical environment. The significance of social learning theory is that it accounts for learned criminal behaviors that are not a result of direct interaction with the immediate environment or interpersonal communication with others.

To explore the social learning perspective in a little more depth we will turn to two of its major proponents in the study of criminal behavior. We begin our discussion with the work of Julian Rotter and then turn to Albert Bandura. We also discuss the significance of Edwin Sutherland's learning theory.

Julian Rotter: Expectancy in Social Learning

According to Rotter (1954, 1972), human behavior depends on expectancy and its reinforcement value. By expectancy, Rotter means "a subjective probability or contingency held by the individual that any specific reinforcement or group of reinforcements will occur in any given situation or situations" (1972:24). Rotter defines reinforcement as "an event that changes the potentiality for occurrence of a given behavior" (1972:17).

Rotter suggests that individuals confront situations with past reinforcement experiences and some general assumptions about probable outcomes of a particular behavior. In other words, individuals size up a situation by relying on past experience and making an assessment of particular outcomes based on value preferences. Rotter (1972) believed that particular behaviors in specific situations could be predicted. Expectancy could be predicted based on decisions a person makes regarding reinforcement contingencies and individual verbal accounts of probable outcomes. However, when an individual's experience results in an unexpected reinforcement, expectations change and new contigencies are added to her/his repertoire (Massey, 1981).

Rotter also notes that reinforcement can have both an internal and external value. Internal reinforcement refers to the individual's understanding and experience of a particular context. External reinforcement deals with the individual's perception of expectant outcomes in relation to a peer group or immediate culture. A particular reinforcement may alter or affect both expectant internal and external behavioral outcomes changing the perceptions of an experience and a group of people (Massey, 1981).

Bartol and Bartol have applied Rotter's concept of expectancy to crime by suggesting that "when people engage in unlawful conduct, they expect to gain something in the form of status, power, affection, material goods, or living conditions" (1986:84). From Rotter's perspective, then, illegal behavior results from certain cognitive expectations held by individuals regarding the consequences of a certain behavior. If unlawful behavior has been reinforced in the past and the immediate situation is favorable to those past conditions, then it is likely that individuals will repeat the behavior. According to Rotter's perspective, individuals commit crime with the expectation of gaining something. The act is carried out by analyzing a particular situation and choosing among courses of action based on cognitive expectations and consequences. Rotter has provided a foundation to social learning theory, but Bandura has expanded its depth and application in the study of crime.

Albert Bandura:
Learning Aggressive Behavior through Observation

The foundation for social learning theory can be found in Rotter's (1954) early work, but the social learning perspective is most often equated with Albert Bandura (Hollin, 1989). Bandura contributed to the study of criminal behavior via experimental research studying the acquisition of aggression by children. Consistent with the learning approaches, Bandura contends that "[p]eople are not born with performed repertoires of aggressive behavior. They must learn them" (1986:200).

Bandura, however, appreciates the effects of biological factors on behavior, but not with the same fervor as Eysenck. Bandura contends that biological dispositions set limits on the types of aggressive behaviors that can be developed and may influence the rate of the learning process (Bandura, 1986:201). Furthermore, he acknowledges that individuals have biological predispositions toward aggressive behavior, "but the activation of these mechanisms depends on appropriate stimulation and is subject to cognitive control" (Bandura, 1986:202). According to Bandura, the modes of aggressive behavior, its frequency, the specific situation, and the locations for attack, are products of socially learned behavior (1986:202). Thus the roles of biology in explaining criminal behavior for Bandura are the limits and stipulations it places on the range of learned behaviors. Therefore, Bandura (1986) contends that social learning is a process of three stages: acquisition, instigation, and maintenance.

Acquisition

For Bandura the social learning process begins at the acquisition stage, which involves the process of observational learning. Bandura (1986) argues that most learning is done vicariously through the observation of others. Through observation the individual learns not only the behavior but the subsequent consequences. According to Bandura, "[t]he capacity to learn by observation enables individuals to acquire large, integrated patterns of behavior without having to form them gradually by tedious trial and error" (1986:202). The significance of this assumption is obvious for Bandura who asks us to think of the fatal outcomes that would plague the survival of our species if behavior were based purely on the consequences of our actions.

Observational learning consists of some basic sub-processes. The first involves the use of attentional processes, which consist of the exploration and perception of observed activities. Another subprocess deals with the importance of memory and its ability to transform "representation into enduring performance guides" (Bandura, 1986:203). Acting upon these symbolic representations created by memory entails the use of motor reproduction processes which allow for the creation of new response patterns. The final subprocess involves the concepts of incentive and motivation. Because all learned behaviors are not performed, some of them may have no functional value or may result in punishment. Thus, whether behaviors learned through observation are carried out depends upon the incentive or motivational process regulating the individual (Bandura, 1986).

Bandura (1973), and Ross and Ross (1961, 1963), have conducted several studies documenting the acquisition of aggressive behaviors by children from adult models. These studies have shown that a child emulates an adult's aggressive behavior, especially when that behavior is rewarded rather than punished. For instance, a child watching adults acting aggressively toward particular props tends to act aggressively, but children who observe passive adults generally act with much less aggression toward objects and others (Bandura, Ross and Ross, 1961). A similar study done with films also found that children imitated the aggressive behavior of the characters, especially when it was rewarded (Bandura, Ross and Ross, 1963).

Bandura (1986) has identified three major sources from which aggressive behavior is acquired through social learning. The first and most obvious is the family. If family members tend to behave toward one another in an aggressive manner, then children are likely to acquire the same aggressive strategies through observation. This is especially true for children whose parents tend to use aggressive solutions to rectify problems or conflicts (Bandura, 1986). Consequently, children that learn such behavior tend to pass it on to their children, creating a vicious cycle of family violence.

The next source from which aggressive behavior may be acquired is the immediate social network which lies just outside the family, such as the influence of subcultures, gangs, neighbors, etc. (Bandura, 1986). Simply put, people in constant contact with aggressive models will eventually utilize what they learn through observation.

The third major source of observationally learned aggressive behavior is mass media. Bandura (1986) cites a myriad of studies which suggest that violence from media sources increases aggressiveness in children and adolescents. He goes on to suggest that the television serves as both a tutor and a model for a host of violent acts and aggressive behaviors that a child without the influence of television would never see. The effect of television violence then is fourfold: "1) It teaches aggressive styles of conduct; 2) it alters restraints over aggressive behavior; 3) it desensitizes and habituates people to violence; and 4) it shapes people's images of reality upon which they base many of their actions" (Bandura, 1986:204).

Bandura's observational learning suggests that most aggressive behavior is acquired through the ability of individuals to discern a number of consequences associated with particular actions. An individual may use aggression in some situations but not in others, suggesting that a host of learned contingencies underlay any behavior. Thus, the acquisition of aggressive behaviors by humans is not purely a mechanistic process like operant conditioning principles suggest. For Bandura, "reinforcement serves principally as an informative and motivational operation rather than as a mechanical response shaper" (1986:207).

Instigation Mechanisms

A social learning theory of aggressive behavior also requires an explanation of motivators or instigators of behavior. Bandura (1986) has identified two sources of motivators for aggressive behavior. The first is biological. Biological motivators deal with physical discomfort caused by either internal deficits or external sources of pain (Bandura, 1986).

The other motivating factors of aggression deal with cognitive construction and representation. Cognitive construction and representation involve the ability of individuals to foresee future consequences before acting. For example, individuals' "outcome expectations may be material (e.g., consummatory, physically painful), sensory (e.g., novel, enjoyable, or unpleasant sensory stimulation), or social (e.g., positive and negative evaluative reactions)" (Bandura, 1986:208). Another dimension of the cognitive process of learning is an individual's ability to set goals and to evaluate her/himself with respect to those goals. Thus how individuals react to situations depends upon how they perceive their behavior in relationship to some goal which can be self evaluated.

Aggression may be provoked by pain but it more often results from "insults, verbal challenges, status threats and unjust treatment" (1986:208). According to Bandura, the way individuals deal with these situations is learned through direct or vicarious experiences. Note that aggression is not based on the psychoanalytical concept of a drive or upon the frustration-aggression hypothesis. For Bandura, aggression is learned, but its provocation comes about through cognitive operations. Individuals define "contexts where it is relatively safe and rewarding to do so, but they are disinclined to act aggressively when aggression carries high risk of punishment" (Bandura, 1986:208). Most aggressive acts, then, are likely to be relative to situations and particular individuals, because they are predicated on a consideration of cognitively generated consequences.

Maintaining Mechanisms

Thus far Bandura's social learning theory of aggression has accounted for how behavior is acquired and motivated. The last aspect of his theory attempts to account for how behaviors are maintained. At this juncture, Bandura (1986) acknowledges the importance of operant conditioning in sustaining aggressive behavior. That is, aggressive behavior can be manipulated by external consequences. For Bandura, however, there exist sources other than traditional operant principles which allow for the reinforcement or maintenance of particular aggressive behaviors. Bandura (1986) also recognizes the significance of vicarious and self-regulatory mechanisms of reinforcement.

By vicarious mechanisms of reinforcement, Bandura means that just as people learn aggressive behavior and its reinforcement value through observing others, they can learn to inhibit their behavior in the same way. Bandura writes:

> Observed outcomes introduce comparative processes into the operation of reinforcement influences. The observed consequences occurring to others provide a standard for judging whether the outcomes one customarily receives are equitable, beneficent, or unfair. The same external outcome can function as a reward or as a punishment depending upon the observed consequences used for comparison. Relational properties of reinforcement affect not only behavior, but the level of personal satisfaction or discontent as well (1986:224).

Vicarious reinforcement provides an explanation for how people can benefit from observing the errors or accomplishments of others without ever acting on the environment.

The other form of reinforcement endemic to the social learning theory of aggression is the use of self-regulating mechanisms. The concept of self-regulating mechanisms is what ultimately differentiates social learning theory from Skinnerian behaviorism. By a self-regulating system, Bandura (1986:225) does not mean a psychic agency like Freud's id, ego or superego which controls behavior: "Rather, it refers to cognitive structures that provide the referential standards against which behavior is judged, and a set of subfunctions for the perception, evaluation, and regulation of action" (Bandura, 1986:225). Self-reinforcement occurs when individuals accomplish goals or conform their behavior to espoused cultural and moral standards. Bandura notes, " [b]y making self-reward and self-punishment contingent on designated performances, people motivate themselves to expand the effort needed to attain performance that gives them self-satisfaction and they refrain from behaving in ways that result in self-censure" (1986:225).

For Bandura, self-reinforcement is undeniably a factor in the perpetuation of violent acts. Bandura (1986) suggests that in some gangs and cultures aggressive behavior is praised. Individuals espousing aggressive gang or cultural values will likely feel heightened feelings of self-worth when engaging in aggressive activities. On the other hand, where individuals have adopted strong standards against aggressive behavior, they are more likely to invoke self-reproach when confronting their aggressive activities (Bandura, 1986). The bottom line is that the more a child perceives and judges an aggressive activity as wrong, the less likely the child will be to perform acts of aggression.

In sum, the importance of Bandura's social learning theory of aggression rests in its concept of vicarious learning and its emphasis on aspects of individual cognition. Bartol and Bartol have noted that the focus on cognition by both Bandura and Rotter have essentially "humanized" the Skinnerian perspective (1986:86). Vicarious learning has provided insights into how individuals learn activities without ever having acted on the environment. The modeling aspects of Bandura's social learning perspective have been widely tested with great success. For a comprehensive review of these studies see Bartol and Bartol, 1986.

Edwin Sutherland: Differential Association Theory

Although not as detailed as Rotter or Bandura, Sutherland's "Differential Association Theory" is included under the social learning rubric because of its emphasis on interaction and interpersonal communication. Because of its lack of detail, however, Sutherland's theory has undergone severe criticisms for the difficulty in operationalizing some of its concepts (Cressey, 1962; Mannheim, 1965; Shoemaker, 1984 Vold and Bernard, 1986;

and for an overview see Martin et al., 1990). This difficulty in operationalizing concepts is what motivated Burgess and Akers (1966) to reformulate Sutherland's theory to comply with operant principles of learning.

We believe, however, that Burgess and Akers' (1966) attempt to restructure Sutherland's theory to read as an operant theory of behavior undermines Sutherland's intentions. Sutherland's historical situation suggests that he knew of Skinner and the work of behaviorists in general. As Martin et al. (1990) have felicitously pointed out, Sutherland and Skinner were at the University of Indiana at the same time. Furthermore, they stress that Skinner published *The Behavior of Organisms* in 1938 and Sutherland's first published manuscript on differential association did not appear until 1939 in *Principles of Criminology* (Martin et al., 1990). Sutherland took a class with behaviorist John B. Watson, which suggests that he was quite aware of the conceptual basis of classical conditioning, but not interested in pursuing the classical or operant perspectives in formulating a theory of crime (Gaylord and Galliher, 1988; Martin et al., 1990).

Halsbach (1979) has suggested that Sutherland's theory has more explanatory power in its original formation than it does as an operant theory. Sutherland's theory provides insight into cognitive aspects of learning, like emotions, motives and attitudes, which operant conditioning theory cannot provide. When comparing the viability of operant theory with social learning, Martin et al. have noted that within the psychology field, the utility of operant and social learning perspectives for explanatory purposes has been debated for quite some time, and "right now it appears that the verdict favors the cognitive social learning interpretations" (1990:167).

Despite contentions that Sutherland's is a purely sociological theory, Martin et al. (1990) have made the most compelling argument in the current literature for treating Sutherland's theory as a social-psychological approach. Martin et al. suggest that "...Sutherland employed a level of abstraction beyond the individual but never totally out of touch with the individual... Sutherland's process involved tracing the development of individuals as they assigned meaning to their experience and to the events in their environment" (1990:148). Sutherland's theory is a product of three levels of analysis (i.e., individual, group, and culture), which makes it extremely significant to sociologists and psychologists alike.

However, according to Bartol and Bartol (1986), Sutherland's theory has been much more popular among social scientists because aspects of Sutherland's theory are somewhat ambiguous with respect to a particular locus of control (i.e., biology or psychology). In addition, they suggest that Sutherland's theory does not identify a particular mode of learning (e.g., classical, operant, or social learning) and it does not deal with different individual abilities to learn (Bartol and Bartol, 1986).

Another major reason for Sutherland's appeal to sociologists is his affinity with the theoretical ideas of the Chicago school. The Chicago school influenced sociological thought from the late nineteenth century through the mid-twentieth century. The Chicago school is famous for contributing three major theoretical explanations of crime: ecological theory, symbolic interactionism, and cultural conflict. Ecological theory contributed to Sutherland's notion of learning by providing a foundation for how deviant values are assimilated in intimate groups. (For an overview of ecological theory see Shoham and Hoffman, 1991).

The second and probably the most influential impact of the Chicago school on Sutherland's theory is the concept of symbolic interactionism. Symbolic interaction is the notion that individuals formulate concepts of themselves through symbolic communication with others. In other words, we create and define ourselves by interacting with others. Symbolic interaction contributed to Sutherland's learning theory by providing the mode of transmission through which rationalizations, motives, drives and attitudes of criminal behavior are learned.

The third influence of the Chicago school on Sutherland's "Differential Association" theory is the idea of conflict. Conflict theory in its simplest form argues that society is comprised of different groups possessing different value systems. The groups with the most power tend to condemn the social values and norms of other, less dominant groups, making them criminal through the creation of laws. Conflict theorists influenced Sutherland by providing his theory with a foundation for why some individuals learn attitudes and behaviors at odds with the law.

The fact that there is a little something for everyone in Sutherland's theory suggests that it is better thought of as a social-psychology theory of crime. Unfortunately, for many the broad scope of Sutherland's theory and its unwillingness to be classified are its most condemning features. For others, however, Sutherland's theory has been extremely important as a heuristic device, which has generated discussion and further investigation into the study of crime (see Martin et al., 1990). Having said this, we offer the basic tenets of Sutherland's theory for the reader to decide its merits as a social-psychology and social learning theory of crime.

The first seven propositions to be presented first appeared in the third edition of Sutherland's 1939 book *Principles of Criminology*. In the 1947 revised fourth edition Sutherland added two more propositions making the theory of "Differential Association" a theory of nine propositions. The first proposition of Sutherland's theory of "Differential Association" reads: "**1) Criminal behavior is learned**" (Sutherland, 1973:8). This proposition, for Sutherland, signifies that criminal behavior is not a biological or psychological predisposition; in other words, there is no such thing as a born criminal. Based on this assumption, Sutherland's theory is an attempt to explain the process by which criminal behavior is acquired.

The second proposition reads: "**2) Criminal behavior is learned in interaction with other persons in a process of communication**" (Sutherland, 1973:8). Sutherland assumes that individuals learn from others through verbal communication and gesturing. Concomitantly, the third proposition reads: "**3) The principle part of the learning of criminal behavior occurs within intimate personal groups**" (Sutherland, 1973:8). Sutherland suggests that most learning is done in interaction with those closest to us. He appears to give little credence to the effect of media sources on learned behavior. This is in direct contradiction with Bandura's (1986) well-supported empirical work on media modeling and imitation.

The fourth proposition reads: "**4) When criminal behavior is learned, the learning includes (a) techniques of committing the crime, which are sometimes very complicated, sometimes very simple; (b) the specific direction of motives, drives, rationalizations, and attitudes**" (Sutherland, 1973:9). This proposition is the most social-cognitive aspect of Sutherland's theory. As Vold and Bernard (1986) have pointed out, this proposition deals with both content and process. It is a process insofar as the criminal technique is elaborately learned. As for content, this proposition provides the context in which individuals construct the meaning of their actions cognitively through communication with others.

Sutherland's fifth proposition states: "**5) The specific direction of motives and drives is learned from definitions of legal codes as favorable and unfavorable**" (Sutherland, 1973:9). It is in this proposition that a social-cognitive basis for self-regulating behavior can be discerned which transcends the external reinforcement dimension of operant conditioning. Individuals learn the moral justifications for their behavior from the group closest to them. This means that an individual could be taught by parents that stealing is wrong and still learn to steal from another group of people which perceives the behavior, in this case stealing, to be morally justifiable. Sutherland does not believe definitions of crime to be universally accepted.

The sixth proposition logically follows the fifth and reads: "**6) A person becomes delinquent because of an excess of definitions favorable to violation of law over definitions unfavorable to violation of law**" (Sutherland, 1973:9). Sutherland refers to this proposition as the principle of "Differential Association." In a quantitative vein, this proposition means that individuals commit crime because they have been exposed to more definitions and patterns favorable to criminal behavior with a measurable absence of noncriminal influences. In a qualitative sense, "[e]xcess refers to the weight of the definitions as determined by the quality and intimacy of the interaction" (Martin et al., 1990:157). Factors that discriminate between the content of behaviors are alluded to in Sutherland's seventh proposition.

The seventh proposition claims: "**Differential associations may vary in frequency, duration, priority, and intensity**" (Sutherland, 1973:9). By frequency Sutherland simply means that the amount of criminal or noncriminal interactions; by duration, he means the quantity and quality of time the individual is exposed to criminal or noncriminal interaction. The concept of priority, on the other hand, is not as easy to operationalize and measure. Sutherland suggests that an individual's behavior may persist through out her/his life (i.e., law-abiding or delinquent). Then again it may not. Sutherland (1973:10) refers to priority as a concept of "selective influence." Priority may best be understood as the element of cognition that allows for rethinking and reassessing attitudes and rationalizations of particular situations. The same line of analysis follows for Sutherland's concept of intensity. He explains, "'[i]ntensity' is not precisely defined, but it has to do with such things as the prestige of the source of a criminal or anti-criminal pattern and with emotional reactions related to the associations" (Sutherland, 1973:10). Sutherland (1973:10) is quite candid about the difficulty in quantifying these concepts.

The eighth proposition contends: "**The process of learning criminal** behavior by association with criminal and anti-criminal patterns involves all of the mechanisms that are involved in any other learning" (Sutherland, 1973:10). This proposition acknowledges and includes within the structure of the theory all the various modes and techniques by which human behavior is learned (i.e., imitation, association, etc.).

The final proposition reads: "Though criminal behavior is an expression of general needs and values, it is not explained by those general needs and values since non-criminal behavior is an expression of the same needs and values" (Sutherland, 1973:100). Sutherland's point here is that it makes no sense to claim that criminal behavior results from basic needs, because the same needs can be shown to drive a law-abiding person's behavior as much as a criminal's. For example, Sutherland (1973:10) suggests that a thief steals money, but an honest laborer works for money. Both individuals need money to survive, so it makes little sense to explain criminal behavior as the result of a person's needing money. The inquiry needs to be directed towards finding out the process and content by which a person learns to becomes a thief.

As noted previously, Sutherland's theory has been the subject of immense empirical study, debate, and criticism. Undeniably, there has not been much empirical support for Sutherland's theory. However, what has evolved from Sutherland's theory is a refinement of concepts which reveal "that the most accurate predictors in criminological prediction research are deducible from differential association theory" (Martin et al., 1990:169). Another important aspect of Sutherland's theory is its multidimensionality and interdisciplinarity, which provide unique ways to view the relationship of the individual to intimate others and to examine how intimate others fare in relation to the larger cultural context.

Overall Criticisms of the Social Learning Perspective

Although all the social learning theorists assert that measurement of internal states is possible, it is the most vulnerable aspect of their theory. As Maddi points out, "[t]o some psychologists, the cognitive, internal, subjective emphasis of social learning theory will indeed brand it as no longer fully scientific" (1980:627). The most ardent critics of social learning theory, then, are likely to be behaviorists. Behaviorists would mount an attack against the notion that an idea or thought could be measured. However, social learning theorists do believe that ideas and thoughts can be subject to measurement through oral and written communication. In short, learning theory, like other personality theories, is amenable to the same tools of testing; hence, aspects of communication (Maddi, 1980).

In fact, much of the work of theorists like Bandura and Rotter has been replicated and found to be extremely sound empirical work (Maddi, 1980). The work of Bandura (1983), Bandura, Ross, and Ross (1963) and Bandura and Walters (1963) on aggression is extremely scientific, meeting the criteria of both predictability and explanation. Bartol and Bartol (1986) have emphasized the explanatory significance and empirical support for the social learning explanation of violent and aggressive behavior. Maddi (1980) also notes that social learning theorists have undermined the belief of behaviorists that all learned behavior can be accounted for based on a system of reward and punishment: social learning theorists have found that behaviors eliciting rewards and punishments can also be learned through observation and imitation.

Behaviorists' criticisms of social learning theorists' inability to empirically test aspects of cognition may not be as damaging to the scientific basis of social learning theory as once thought. That is, concepts and propositions of social learning theory are easily testable and in many cases have been found to provide extremely sound empirical observations of the learning process. On the other hand, it is doubtful that the more subtle dimensions of thinking and information processing can ever be fully understood, by virtue of the fact that we as humans are both the subjects and objects of inquiry. Nevertheless, expanding and refining our understanding of internal mental processes is a popular subject of inquiry as we will see in the next chapter on cognitive psychology.

SUMMARY

In this chapter, we have explored the modification of learning theories in psychology and how these theories have been used in the study of crime. Our discussion of learning theory began with classical conditioning. Classical conditioning is a theory of learning which suggests criminal behavior is learned through association. The subject, in classical conditioning, is perceived as extremely passive and criminal behavior results from reacting to certain stimuli. From this perspective, to act criminal is in essence the natural response of a human subject.

The second form of learning discussed in this chapter deals with operant conditioning. In operant conditioning subjects commit crimes because they learn that a response to a stimulus leads to a consequence. In other words, stealing money leads to the ability to buy more material possessions. If the behavior of stealing is continuously reinforced, then it is likely to persist. In order to relinquish a behavior, the removal of a reinforcement or the creation of an aversive stimulus to discourage the particular behavior is necessary.

The final form of learning discussed in this chapter is social learning. Social learning incorporates both classical and operant conditioning dimensions in its scope, but also adds an internal dimension to the process of learning. Social learning theory accounts for those criminal behaviors that are not linked to a direct interaction with the immediate environment or to interpersonal communication with others. Individuals can, in effect, form hypotheses about future events. As such, people can imagine themselves stealing clothes from a store and also foresee both the reward and the punishment for such a behavior, before actually committing the act of theft.

Although all three of these perspectives account for aspects of criminal behavior, it appears that social learning theory may be the most powerful with respect to explanation and possibly prediction. Social learning theory is more versatile when it comes to accounting for the complexity of many human behaviors. In fact, social learning theory has paved the way for the study of more complex dimensions of human behavior and has provided the foundation for cognitive perspectives on crime.

Five

Cognitive Learning Perspectives

STUDYING CRIMINAL behavior from a cognitive perspective entails inquiring into an individual's mental activity, specifically thinking (e.g., intelligence and meaning construction), decision making, and perceptions of self and others. In short, cognitive psychology deals with how individuals perceive, organize and construct meaning from information. It looks at aspects of an individual's history and how aspects of that history mediate that individual's experiences (Mischel, 1973).

Aside from psychoanalysis, all the psychological perspectives we have discussed thus far have either emerged from the modification or the outright rejection of another perspective's assumptions. The cognitive perspective is no exception. In general, it rejects the mechanical stimulus-response laws of radical behaviorism, the concept of fixed trait dispositions, and the internal dimensions characteristic of psychoanalytic theory.

Behaviorism cannot adequately account for the process by which complex behaviors are learned. For example, flying an airplane, learning to read, and writing an opera are complex activities which transcend the explanatory power of the stimulus- response laws endemic to behaviorism (Gagne, 1985). In addition, cybernetic theory (the study of systems) and the research that has taken place in linguistics (see Chomsky, 1959) have cast considerable doubt on traditional behaviorist/operant approaches used to explain complex types of learning.

Cognitive personality theorists also reject global trait theories. They study the conditions under which individual behaviors are evoked and modified. Trait theorists, on the other hand, tend to compare and generalize behaviors between individuals without concern for the situation in which individuals interact; they tend to treat individuals as though they possess immutable dispositions. For cognitive theorists, Mischel asserts: "[t]he focus shifts from describing situation-free people with broad trait adjectives to analyzing the specific interactions between conditions and the cognitions and behaviors of interest" (1973:265).

Cognitive theorists are also critical of psychoanalytical claims that unconscious forces control behavior. The idea that reality exists mostly in an internal state does not sit well with them. Cognitive theorists perceive stimuli from the environment and the individual's cognitive internal state as part of a continuous process of reciprocal interaction, each modifying the other to meet the circumstances of a particular situation.

At the core, then, of cognitive personality theories is the assumption that individuals possess internal predispositions in their ability to process information and give it meaning. The more active an individual's cognition, the more the individual can construct events in her/his world, which allows for greater control over self and the reinforcing influences of the external environment (Maddi, 1980). Although social situations are important, they cannot be the sole predictor of behavior because individuals cognitively construe situations differently.

In the study of crime, cognitive theory has been concerned with aspects of thinking, perceptions of self, and the decision making process of individuals involved in criminal behavior. For example, if two individuals have the same opportunity to commit a crime, one may commit a crime while the other may not. Cognitive theory attempts to explain why some individuals make the choices they do in relation to their perception and understanding of situations.

Before exploring this area further, however, it is necessary to explore how this focus of study developed. This chapter will begin with a brief discussion of cognitive developmental theories and social-cognitive learning theories. A section discussing rational choice models and the symbolic interactionist perspective as early cognitive explorations in the study of crime will follow. Finally, some of the more contemporary cognitive perspectives on crime will be explored.

Aspects of Cognitive Psychology

One of the most important dimensions of cognitive study is the developmental aspect. The developmental aspect explores ways in which humans' mental abilities evolve to perform complex tasks like reasoning, and contemplating ethical decisions and moral issues. Jean Piaget (1952), a Swiss psychologist, conducted the first intensive studies of the cognitive abilities of children. Piaget constructed a heuristic model of child development based on age and complexity of tasks. He reasoned that a general framework of childhood socialization could be mapped out showing each subsequent advancement in chronological age with its advancement in cognitive abilities. For example, at age two children learn to differentiate themselves from objects, from age two to seven children acquire language, from age seven to twelve children learn to think logically about events and objects, and after age 12 children learn to think abstractly about propositions and hypotheses (Atkinson et al., 1981).

Accompanying the advancement of cognitive abilities in children is what Kohlberg (1969, 1973) described as cognitive advancement in moral development. Based upon the work of Piaget, Kohlberg argued that children develop a sense of morality and ethical concerns based upon their intellectual capacities. For instance, Kohlberg (1969) thought there were six basic stages or three levels of moral development. The first level is preconventional morality, which consists of two stages. The first stage is punishment oriented and entails obeying rules to avoid punishment. At the second stage a person conforms to laws or rules with the expectation of some sort of reward.

The second level, referred to as conventional morality by Kohlberg, contains stages three and four of moral development. Kohlberg (1969) describes the third stage as the "good person syndrome," when the individual conforms to avoid the disapproval of others. At the fourth stage individuals uphold the laws and rules of society because they fear censorship and guilt about not performing "one's duty." Kohlberg (1969) feels most people never progress beyond level two.

Level three, postconventional morality, consists of stages five and six. Stage five is a social contract orientation, based on a thorough understanding of the importance of agreed upon rules and laws for the purpose of the public welfare, mutual and self respect. The sixth and final stage, which Kohlberg (1969) suggests is characteristic of only 10 percent of the population over 16 years of age, deals with ethical principles. At this level humans behave according to self-chosen ethical principles which tend to value concepts of equality and justice.

It should be noted that Kohlberg's last two stages of moral development have been severely criticized as extremely ethnocentric (Snarey, 1987). One of the major problems with constructing a developmental model of moral development like Kohlberg's is the element of cultural relativity. One person's idea of justice and equality may be someone else's idea of injustice and inequality (compare the moral ideologies of the US and China). In other words, Kohlberg's description of the highest moral levels are only the epitome of the Western world's value system.

Kohlberg also suggested that women tend to make moral decisions differently than men do. He assumed, as did many of his predecessors, that females were deficient in moral character. Carol Gilligan (1982) has produced research that contradicts Kohlberg's assumptions by suggesting that women take a different set of values and premises to a situation, which accounts for different moral reasoning. Gilligan's (1982) research, however, has also been criticized for implicit assumptions about male/female cognitive differences rather than difference based in the socialization process (Snarey, 1987). Most studies find no difference in cognitive abilities between women and men (Snarey, 1987).

Nevertheless, Kohlberg's theory of moral development has been explored more peripherally than directly in the study of criminal behavior. Cognitive studies of criminal behavior have tended to focus on how certain types of individuals construe their situation based upon their cognitive abilities. For example, individuals capable of greater abstract thought and insight tend to be less apt to choose a violent solution to potentially problematic situations (Heilbrun, 1982; Martin, 1985).

Cognitive-Social Learning Theorists

Rotter (1954), Bandura, (1962, and Mischel (1973) form another part of the foundation to a cognitive focus of study. In fact, these theorists once referred to as social learning theorists are now recognized as the founders of cognitive social learning theory (Bartol and Bartol, 1986; Massey, 1981; Maddi 1980). Their contribution to cognitive theory was to shift the locus of learning theory from purely environmental conditions to an emphasis upon the integration of external environment and internal factors. They contend that most learning takes place without a person actually acting on the environment; that is, without a person responding to a negative or positive reinforcement (see Rotter 1954; Bandura, 1962, 1986 [1979]; Mischel, 1973). These theorists have shown that memory and perception are measurable through oral and written forms, even though they are not tangible (see Maddi, 1980).

Rotter's (1954) contribution to cognitive theory is his contention that behavior is a result of an expected reinforcement. To reiterate from Chapter Four, "expectant reinforcement" means that a person's values and expectancies about a situation are internal mental events which interact to produce a behavior. Rotter's emphasis becomes uniquely cognitive when one considers that the locus of control lies purely in the individual's interpretation of reality. In other words, each individual is going to formulate different perceived values and expectancies about situations confronting her/him. Empirical confirmation of Rotter's perspective is based upon the ability to predict a particular individual's behavior rather than the behavior of aggregate populations.

Bandura's contribution to cognitive theory is his assertion that learning in humans occurs more through imitation and modeling than operant conditioning. It is suggested by Bandura's (1986) experiments with children that learning is a sophisticated process of information processing and decision making based on perceived future outcomes. Although Bandura recognizes the significance of internal functions in the process of learning, he is more concerned with the situational factors which contribute to the way certain behaviors are learned. He does not concern himself with elaborate descriptions of how each individual processes information based upon their own perceptions of the world (for a more comprehensive discussion of Bandura, see Chapter Four).

Another important cognitive social learning theorist is Walter Mischel

(1973, 1979), who has brought person variables into interaction with cognitive competencies and situational factors. While Mischel was not concerned specifically with the study of crime, he has made an important contribution in the focus of cognitive studies. Mischel (1973) has outlined five critical areas of person variables which have been used indirectly to study violence and criminal behavior. These areas are: "cognitive and behavioral construction competencies; encoding strategies and personal constructs; behavior-outcome and stimulus outcome; subjective stimulus values; and, self regulatory systems" (Mischel, 1973:265). .

By cognitive and behavioral construction competencies Mischel means the various operations and transformations that an individual performs on information (1973:266). This area of personality study operates from the assumptions that individuals store a large volume of information acquired through direct and observational learning. Mischel notes, "it is apparent that each individual acquires the capacity to construct a great range of potential behaviors and different individuals acquire different behavior construction capabilities" (1973:266). Indicators of behavioral and cognitive competencies are measurable dimensions of social and intellectual maturity, IQ, and ego development. This area of personality study suggests those individuals who have a wider range of organized information to draw from are likely to be more able to adjust to a variety of situations. As we will see, there is substantial support for this conclusion in some criminal behavior studies.

Encoding strategies and personal constructs refer to the ways individuals group information from stimulus inputs (Mischel, 1973:267). This area of personality study focuses on how individuals select certain stimuli over others, interpret the stimuli, and categorize them in particular ways. The focus here is on why certain stimuli produce different effects on different individuals. This process needs to be understood as a reciprocal information transfer; the individual brings information to the stimuli while simultaneously receiving information from the stimuli. Some individuals, for example, will focus on the shape of an object while the others pay more attention to its color. Why? Likewise, one person may perceive a particular situation as a threat, whereas another person perceives it as an ordinary encounter.

The third aspect of study outlined by Mischel (1973) regarding cognitive personality variables is "behavior-outcome and stimulus-outcome expectancies." Mischel accentuates the significance of Rotter's line of inquiry. This dimension of study deals with the actual behavior of the individual— the transition from perceived courses of action to an actual behavior. Expectancy, as a person variable, is important because many individuals respond to identical situations with different expectations. Cognitive psychology, then, also studies individual expectancies based on each persons own unique experiences and information base (Mischel, 1973).

Another area important to cognitive study, according to Mischel (1973), is "subjective stimulus values". Individuals sharing the same expectancies may still produce different behaviors in a particular situation. In this case, the difference in the behaviors may be linked to what Mischel refers to as different subjective values. Mischel refers to subjective values as "stimuli that have acquired the power to induce positive or negative emotional states in the person and to function as incentives or reinforcers for his [sic] behavior" (1973:273). Subjective values induced by stimuli may change in relation to different experiences, or through educational modes; they are not fixed responses to stimuli (Mischel, 1973).

The final area of cognitive study identified by Mischel (1973) is self-regulatory systems. This area has been an important focus of study in social learning theory as explicated in the last chapter by Bandura (1986). The concept of individuals as self-regulating systems deals with how people control their own behavior by creating standards and criteria for evaluating those standards. Mischel suggests, "[s]uch rules specify the kinds of behavior appropriate (expected) under particular conditions, the performance levels (standards, goals) which the behavior must achieve, and the consequences (positive or negative) of attaining or failing to reach those standards" (1973:274). In short, the study of self-regulating cognitive dimensions of behavior deals with how individuals devise internal strategies to regulate behavior in the absence or in defiance of external pressures.

Rotter's concept of expectancy, Bandura's work on observation and imitation, and Mischel's application of these approaches to a theory of personality has provided a framework in which cognitive theory has gained some appeal in the study of crime. As Clarke and Cornish (1985) have pointed out, however, social learning theory is not the sole contributor to the study of cognition in criminal behavior. Rational choice models and symbolic interactionist perspectives have contributed to the refinement of a general cognitive emphasis in the psychology of crime.

Although not as detailed as many contemporary approaches to cognitive studies, there have been many criminology theories that broke with pure environmental determinism and focused on aspects of individual decision making and choice. These theoretical traditions have cognitive dimensions and are the earliest attempts in the study of crime to acknowledge the importance of information processing and decision making. Our discussion will now turn to some of these earlier theoretical traditions.

Early Conceptions of Cognition in the Study of Crime

The earliest perspectives in criminology dealing with human beings as rational information processors and decision makers date back to the writings of Beccaria (1963 [1764]) and Bentham (1948), who are often credited as the founders of the classical school of criminology (for a comprehensive review of the classical school see Vold and Bernard, 1986). These theorists viewed human beings as rational, calculating creatures, who choose their courses of action based on the analysis of consequences. The concept of deterrence comes from the belief that individuals calculate their actions in relation to the amount of pleasure and pain they might encounter. If the pleasure of committing a crime outweighs the pain, an individual will choose criminal action. Like the behaviorists, many rational choice theorists suggest that individuals make decisions based on the expectation of rewards. The differentiating factor, however, is the concept of choice (Clarke and Cornish, 1985).

A basic criticism of these older rational choice models is that they do not take into consideration individual differences that enter into the decision making process (Cook, 1980; Clark and Cornish, 1985; Gottfredson and Hirschi, 1990). From a theoretical and policy standpoint, ignoring individual differences in decision making makes it difficult to determine who is going to choose crime and why. Cook (1980) has attempted to deal with this issue, as have Gottfredson and Hirschi (1990), by focusing upon individual elements. For Cook (1980), the focus has been on the process of the individual's subjective evaluation of the situation; for Gottfredson and Hirschi (1990), the issue has been identifying traits of self-control that serve as predictors of how an individual will make choices in particular situations.

Despite these latter attempts to clarify and empirically strengthen rational choice models, cognitive psychology has gone beyond the basic premise of rational choice, or at least expanded the parameters in which a decision is judged rational. For example, many cognitive studies have found that individuals of all different backgrounds and occupations do not always make choices that are in their best interest (Cornish, 1978; Clark and Cornish, 1985; Kozielecki, 1982). Or, some individuals may perceive their choices and decisions as rational, while to others their choices seem irrational (see Clarke and Cornish, 1985:158-61).

Other theoretical models dealing with aspects of cognition in the study of crime have been more sociological in nature. One of the most comprehensive reviews in the criminological literature dealing with the rational dimension and decision making abilities of individuals is by Clarke and Cornish (1985). Clarke and Cornish build their own cognitive model of decision making on earlier sociological works dealing with the decision process in assimilating deviant roles. They cite such instrumental works as Howard Becker's (1963) study on marijuana use among jazz singers, Matza's (1964) study dealing with "delinquency, drift and neutralization," Taylor, Walton and Young's book titled the *New Criminology* (1973), and Gibbs and Shelly's (1982) study of theft as a means to living in the fast lane. All these works emphasize the subject's role in rationalizing and formulating the context and purpose for their deviant behavior.

One of the most influential theoretical camps studying deviant self constructs and situational definitions is the symbolic interactionist group. Symbolic interactionists deal with how meaning is transferred through interactions with others. They believe the process of meaning construction to be dynamic, involving an interplay of feedback from interpersonal relations and an individual's own subjective decisions and judgments. Through this reciprocal process of information transfer between the subjective and the social environment, a social self is formed and maintained (see Pfuhl, 1986; Becker, 1973).

The social deviance and interactionist camps have provided some interesting insights into individual criminality with respect to attitudes and particular life-styles. However, Clark and Cornish point out that the interactionist and social deviance approaches lack crime control policy relevance and sound methodological and quantitative rigor (1985:152). This criticism may be valid from Clark and Cornish's perspective, but these same criticisms may also be applied to many contemporary cognitive studies as well. Theorists who focus on individuals and their unique cognitive abilities will usually have difficulty formulating sweeping crime control policies aimed at controlling aggregate populations.

THE APPLICATION OF COGNITIVE PSYCHOLOGY IN THE STUDY OF CRIME

Clark and Cornish (1985) note that the application of cognitive psychology to the study of crime has been rather limited. They contend that "cognitive psychology is still at an early stage in its development and the topics studied so far are not necessarily those that best illuminate criminal decision making" (Clarke and Cornish, 1985:160). Hollin (1989) notes that cognition is an imprecise term, hence it appears in a variety of forms in the criminal behavior literature. Because the application of cognitive theory in the study of crime is both limited and diverse, the remainder of this section will focus on three broadly defined areas of cognitive study: thinking processes, self-concept, and decision making.

Thinking Processes and Crime

There are many variables that contribute to an individual's ability to think. These variables range from basic intelligence to an individual's ability to empathize, synthesize information, control impulses, and regulate conduct according to the norms and values of society. Obviously, the context of thinking in the human mind is extremely sophisticated. Overall, modern science knows very little about the functioning of the brain. Thus, research making comprehensive claims about thinking patterns requires careful scrutiny.

Some cognitive criminal psychologists have suggested that criminals possess different thinking patterns (Yochelson and Samenow, 1976; Samenow, 1983; Samenow, 1984). In fact, Yochelson and Samenow (1976) claim to have found the basic thought patterns that characterize the criminal's mind. Based on 240 clinical interviews with criminals and the criminally insane, Yochelson and Samenow (1976) claim to have identified 52 different forms of criminal thinking patterns. For example, the criminal mind may exhibit patterns like impulsiveness, concrete thinking, lack of empathy, fragmentation, suspiciousness, sensation seeking, lack of a conception of time, and manipulativeness (Yochelson and Samenow, 1976).

Yochelson and Samenow (1976) make some bold claims, which have been subject to scathing criticism aimed at their methodology (Jacoby, 1977; Hollin, 1989; Nietzel, 1979; Ross and Fabiano, 1985; Vold, 1979). An obvious shortcoming in Yochelson and Samenow's (1976) work is their use of a sample of 240 criminally insane or criminal offenders with no control group (Hollin, 1989). In addition to these criticisms, Ross and Fabiano (1985) have suggested that research claims of a definitive type (i.e., criminal mind) create more controversy than valued science.

One of the most employed variables in the study of crime has been the concept of individual intelligence. As was noted in Chapter Three, many social scientists studying criminal behavior have used intelligence as a psychological trait predictive of criminal behavior. Heilbrun (1979, 1982) has explored intelligence as a cognitive variable indicative of "the quality of information processing available to the criminal" (1982:547). In one study, Heilbrun (1979) indicates that intelligence influences the relationship between psychopathy and violence. In other words, the lower the intelligence (IQ measure) among psychopathic personalities, the greater likelihood they will be violent. The findings suggest an important link for which the literature was unable to account until Heilbrun's 1979 study. Hielbrun's findings suggest that those meeting psychopathy profiles, as determined from the Minnesota Multiphasic Personality Inventory (MMPI), do not possess higher violent crime rates compared to those having no psychopathic tendencies. In other words, intelligent psychopathic personalities tend to be less violent than less intelligent psychopathic personalities; this trend lowers the violent crime rates among those considered to possess psychopathic personalities. Heilbrun's (1979) study suggests that intelligence is an important factor in determining the way individuals process and act upon information, especially whether or not they will act violently.

In a follow-up study, Heilbrun (1982) looks at some additional, but specific, cognitive variables and their relation to intellectual functioning and psychopathy. The cognitive variables consisted of impulse control, strategies of self reinforcement, and empathy. Heilbrun's study found the following:

> Both cognitive control of impulses and empathy require effective processing of information, and both were found to be diminished in the less intelligent criminal. Thus, the prior finding of high risk for

violence in the low-IQ psychopath can be partially explained in terms of two cognitive deficits commonly assumed to characterize the psychopathic personality. The combination of poor cognitive control and insensitivity to others' feelings, associated with limited intelligence, appear in themselves to be conducive to violent behavior (1982:553).

Heilbrun (1982) also reports that intelligent psychopaths are less likely to be impulsive.

Studies dating back to Glueck and Glueck's (1950) research have asserted that impulsiveness plays an important role in criminal behavior. The explanation has been that people who lack self control tend to be impulsive (Glueck and Glueck, 1950; Ahlstrom and Havinghurst, 1971; Gottfredson and Hirschi, 1990). Ross and Fabiano (1985) have noted that impulsive people lack a certain degree of reflection in particular situations. In other words, impulsive individuals do not perform a cognitive analysis of particular situations, they do not review alternative courses of action in their thinking, nor do they process the various possible outcomes of their actions.

The following cognitive studies suggest that criminal behavior, especially violence, may be the result of a particular individual's inability to perceive alternative courses of action in her/his thinking process. This inability to construe a situation in a variety of ways appears to be linked to some sort of cognitive deficit. Heilbrun's (1982) research has suggested that intelligence (as measured by IQ) influences whether an individual is impulsive or empathetic. The study by Freedman et al. (1978) has delineated several different types of deficits in social skills of delinquent and nondelinquent boys. Studies by Platt et al. (1973) and Higgins and Thies (1981) have also noted deficits in problem solving skills (i.e., the inability to generate options and solutions). Taken together, this research suggests that because some individuals have difficulty understanding the complexity of social situations and alternative courses of action, they end up as offenders. For example, someone who robs another individual fails to understand the fear and humiliation suffered by that individual. Punching somebody in the face for looking at your date may reflect an inability to cognitively construe situations in a wider context.

While these studies provide some evidence that there are tangible differences between delinquent and nondelinquent adolescents in social cognitive ability, Hollin (1989) has suggested that we must be cautious in regarding the validity of the measures used and in interpreting the functional relationships of cognition. In short, it is difficult to establish "the process by which the cognition results in offending" (Hollin, 1989:49).

Some cognitive theorists, who have studied the thinking patterns of individuals committing criminal behavior and gratuitous violence, have concentrated upon the interaction of intelligence with commonly espoused, trait-like attributes (e.g., empathy, impulsiveness, etc.). Others have attempted to explicate the difference between delinquents and nondelinquents regarding social skills, especially those needed in problem solving. All told, this dimension of cognitive study has attempted to discover different modes of thinking patterns between offender and non-offender populations by emphasizing the deficit in cognitive skills of the delinquent and violent offender.

Self-Concept and Cognition

Research dealing with self-concept and cognition has focused on locus of control (Hollin, 1989) and perceptions of self and others (Johnson, 1972; Toch, 1969, 1977, 1986 [1979]; Martin, 1985). The research emphasis surrounding the former focuses on individual perceptions of control. It explores how individuals attribute their behavioral actions to internal or external forces. For instance, one study conducted by Kumchy and Sayer (1980) purported that offenders tend to explain their behavior as a result of external forces. Other studies have found no difference between offender and non-offender populations (see Hollin, 1989). There are also several studies which contend that individuals perceive internal or external controlling factors in their behavior based on the context of particular situations like politics, race, or type of crime (see Hollin, 1989 for a review of this literature).

A major problem in research dealing with locus of control is that it operates on the assumption that "offenders form a homogeneous population" (Hollin, 1989:49). An overall summary of the locus of control research suggests "[i]f locus of control does have some relationship with offending, it will require rather more sophisticated research than is presently available to discover its exact role" (Hollin, 1989:49).

The other dimension of self-concept deals explicitly with how individuals committing antisocial behaviors perceive themselves. Some studies have suggested that self-concept may play a major role in the lives of those exhibiting violent and various other antisocial behaviors (see especially, Johnson, 1972; Toch, 1969, 1977; Newman, 1979; Martin, 1985). Research by Wolfgang and Ferracuti (1967) and Newman (1979) suggests that violence is not a factor endemic to all criminal populations. In Toch's 1969 study of violence he constructed a self-evaluation classification system for examining offenders' justifications for committing violent acts. His study emphasizes the coping strategies adopted by violent persons in situations they consider to be threatening. For instance, Toch (1969) points to how some violence may result from a need to promote or defend one's self image. Toch's "self-image promoter is a man who works hard at manufacturing the impression that he is not to be trifled with— that he is formidable and fearless" 1969:137). His violence is designed to impress both the victim and the potential audience. This show of force dispels any myth that this person is weak, or worse yet, a coward (Toch, 1969:137). Toch's "self-image defender is a man who is extremely sensitive to the implications of other people's actions to his integrity, manliness, or worth" (1969:144). This person's "violence arises in the form of responses to challenges, retaliations to slights, or reactions against aspersions to his advertised self-conception" (Toch, 1969:144).

Toch's (1969) classification system is a typology for understanding coping strategies of violent men facing potentially conflictual situations more than it is an individual self-concept assessment. Because Toch's (1969) study is focused on violence, he does not explore the notion of self-concept for violent men outside the particular tumultuous context of the one-on-one interaction. Nevertheless, Toch's notion of self-concept and its relation to violent behavior is important.

There have been some studies that have looked directly at measures of self-concept within the incarcerated population. Martin (1985) studied 38 male inmates who had committed both assaultive and nonassaultive offenses, and found that differences in self-concept exist between assaultive and nonassaultive populations. Martin describes the assaultive inmate profile as a person who has "a somewhat over-inflated self concept, a lack of discriminability in evaluating self and others" (1985:8). Martin goes on to suggest that violent persons lack an ability to engage in abstract thought which prevents them from discerning multiple issues involved in complex social situations. This assessment was made on the basis of data from cognitive/moral development measures given to the inmates, on which many of them scored below the norm for their age group (Martin , 1985).

Inability in these areas also leads to a lack of empathy (Martin, 1985). Individuals lacking interactive and perceptual skills are much more likely to perceive social options as either/or situations. For example, something as simple as an ambiguous facial gesture from person A may be interpreted by person B as an attack on her/his dignity and a justification for violence; even though person A was thinking about something entirely unrelated to person B. In sum, Martin's (1985) findings suggest that those assaultive individuals with a high self-regard, and who have in the past used violence as a solution to the either/or dilemma, have little problem rationalizing violent acts.

Ronald Farrell (1989) has constructed an integrated theory that explores a cognitive conception of ambiguity tolerance. Building on the symbolic interactionist, strain, and cultural models, Farrell (1989) attempts to provide an understanding of individual difference with respect to the construction of meaning and the labeling effect. He contends that these theories have greatly contributed to the complex process of deviance, but have failed to adequately account for similarly situated individuals pursuing different courses of action. Farrell's (1989) perspective is an attempt to incorporate an attribute of personality called ambiguity tolerance into the interactionist framework to account for the different courses of action similarly situated individuals pursue.

Ambiguity tolerance "refers to the degree to which persons accept uncertainty and the subjectivity of meaning" (Farrell, 1989:82). In other words, individuals who feel uneasy about ambiguity need structure, and confine themselves by this need to making absolute decisions about social experience (Farrell, 1985). "They have fixed cognitive categories and tend to avoid situations that contradict their beliefs" (Farrell, 1985:82). Individuals who deal with experience in this way tend to find complex social situations extremely threatening. In the same vein, however, those who express higher levels of tolerance for ambiguity may find such situations comfortable and even desirable (Farrell, 1989).

According to Farrell (1989), the individual's ability to tolerate ambiguity is going to determine the effectiveness of the labeling process. He contends:

> that the relative need to reconstruct one's situation in accordance with

the social response is determined by the individual's ability to tolerate ambiguity. Those unable to tolerate ambiguity are more likely to unequivocally define their behavior or attributes as stereotypically deviant, to interpret more literally the definitions and responses of others, and to experience the dissonance and need to resolve the conflicting cognitive elements surrounding the deviation (Farrell, 1989:85).

Thus, individuals succumbing to deviant labels (e.g., thief, drug addict, etc.) do so out of necessity to maintain their cognitive equilibrium. In other words, the conflict between grappling with the pressure of societal reaction to their deviance and the need to have some stable conception of self may force individuals to accept stereotypical responses to their behavior.

A practical example of Farrell's theoretical perspective would be something along these lines. There are many casual users of marijuana who do not consider themselves drug addicts. Say for example, that a couple of these casual users get arrested for the second time in the same year for smoking marijuana. One of these casual users is very intolerant of ambiguity (person A) and the other is quite tolerant of ambiguity (person B). Person A may find the societal pressure regarding drug use and the stigma attached to his behavior to be simply cognitively inundating. Person A's friends do not smoke marijuana and they are beginning to question his continued smoking and trouble with the law. Person A's friends begin to treat him differently. As a result, person A begins to find himself mired in self conflict with respect to his identity. Because person A cannot handle this identity ambiguity, he begins to espouse the label (i.e., drug addict), its stigma, and begins to associate with a more deviant group, bringing his psychological constitution back into equilibrium.

Person B on the other hand, mediates the effect of the label and societal pressures so they do not conflict with her identity. Person B is less likely to take the label of drug addict as a literal definition of who she is. Person B realizes the context of the situation and is less dependant upon group approval to validate her actions. In short, Person B perceives herself as a person who likes to smoke marijuana, but also enjoys reading philosophy, writing poetry and playing music. Person B's self-esteem is not subject to the societal influences and stigma that person A's is, because person B is much more tolerant of ambiguity and complex situations.

Farrell's (1985) integrated theory has brought together the sociological phenomenon of labeling and added to it the psychological dimension of individual cognition, which accounts for the differentiation of the labeling effect on different individuals. Cognitive research on self-concept has greatly aided our understanding of individuals who rationalize violence and are able to justify criminal activity. Despite this, however, there are many criminals and violent people who are very intelligent and hold rather high concepts of themselves. The lack of knowledge in this area suggests uncharted ground for future researchers interested in studying the dynamics of self.

Cognitive Decision Making and Crime

The cognitive decision making models dealing with criminality are relatively new and lack a history of theory generation and research support. Nevertheless, there are some criminal decision making models in the literature for those who have special interest in a particular crime. For instance, Cornish (1978) conducted a study on decision making among gamblers. Walsh (1978, 1980) has studied the decision making process regarding burglary. Carrol (1982) has done cognitive studies dealing with offenders' decisions to commit a crime and Carrol and Weaver (1986) have conducted a study on the decision process involved in shoplifting. Cornish and Clarke (1986) have surveyed several studies conducted on the decision process used in particular crimes ranging from illicit drug use (Bennet, 1986), to robbery (Feeney, 1986), to the decision process involved in ending criminal careers (Cusson and Pinsonnealut, 1986). The most extensive effort to bring to the forefront cognitive decision making models for further research and policy is the work of Clarke and Cornish (1985).

Clarke and Cornish (1985) suggest that criminal decision making models have to incorporate a variety of factors. Criminal decision models need to consider not only individual dispositions, but the situational context and the various stages by which criminals become involved in a criminal action. Clarke and Cornish (1985) point out that initial involvement in some criminal activity (e.g., vandalism, shoplifting) may occur without much reflection and forethought. The decision, however, to continue or desist with a criminal activity involves much more complexity. After individuals have committed an offense, they acquire a certain knowledge about the consequences of the offense, which results in the behavior continuing or desisting. Clarke and Cornish argue that this knowledge may "provide the background of experience to render initial involvement in another crime a considered choice" (1985:164).

Another important factor emphasized by Clarke and Cornish (1985) is the importance of crime specific models. They contend that decision models need to emphasize the important difference between crimes, the motivations, and the various behaviors required. They go so far as to suggest that burglary as a type of crime may be too broad of a category and should be broken down into different types of burglary (e.g., residential, industrial, etc.). In fact, one of the decision models that Clarke and Cornish (1985) provide entails an analysis of the individual decision process in committing a residential burglary.

To illustrate their position, Clarke and Cornish (1985) construct a criminal decision making model regarding residential burglary in a middle class neighborhood. In a model specifying eight stages, Clarke and Cornish (1985) suggest that the last two stages are the most important. These two stages are the individual's readiness to commit a particular offense and the actual decision to commit the burglary. By readiness they mean that the individual has fully contemplated the crime of burglary as a solution to satisfy her/his need for money, goods or excitement.

According to Clarke and Cornish (1985), by the time the decision to commit the burglary has been made, the individual has evaluated several different courses of action which could also satisfy her/his needs. Clarke and Cornish suggest that the individual will draw heavily on past learned experiences, and will have considered "his [sic] moral code, his view of the kind of person he is, his personal and vicarious experiences of crime, and the degree to which he can plan and exercise foresight" (1985:167). They also point out that these factors are related to social background factors like family situation, gender, education, and class. While Clarke and Cornish consider these factors important, they acknowledge that these are the only factors with which criminology has been preoccupied. Rather than seeing these factors as predetermining an individual's criminality, Clarke and Cornish (1985) see these factors has having only an "orienting function." In other words, these background factors present the array of possibilities and outcomes, but they do not constitute the decision to act. Clarke and Cornish go so far as to suggest that these background factors are even more mediated by the situation and immediate influences confronting the individual at the time she or he decides to commit the crime.

The second major decision point which leads to actually committing the burglary involves a chance event. They reveal that "the two decision points may occur almost simultaneously and the chance event may not only precipitate the decision to burgle, but may also play a part in the precipitation and evaluation of solutions to generalized needs" (Clarke and Cornish, 1985:168-169). At this juncture a decision to burgle requires a host of other decisions (e.g., which house to burgle). Clarke and Cornish (1985) go on to elaborate on the various decision stages that are made throughout the duration of the burglary as well as the decision process to continue being a professional burglar.

In sum, decision making in cognitive theory emphasizes the importance of the whole process of committing a criminal act. This process entails the personal background factors of the individual, a consideration of individual personal experiences, needs, moral framework, the readiness to commit a crime, and the actual situation which allows for the crime to be committed. The entire process is interrelational and interactional. An offender's disposition alone does not provide the sole impetus to a criminal act. The situation must also be considered in its entirety. Throughout the entire process, the individual must be considered an active participant using reason and judgment to guide her/his choice to commit a criminal act. Thus social background, personal variables, and situational factors must be considered together as an interactive process which leads to a criminal decision.

The major problem with decision making models are their lack of generalizability in terms of providing effective strategies leading to crime prevention. Clarke and Cornish (1985) make the argument that by focusing on very specific definitions of particular crimes and by breaking the criminal event down into all of its constituent parts, a profile of an offender's characteristics will merge with a particular type of offense. That is, a person who vandalizes will have characteristics different from an individual who assaults. At this time, however, the evidence suggesting that most criminals are specialists is weak. In fact, studies on career criminals suggest that offenders may be more generalists in the choice of their crimes than specialists.

Another issue is the diversity of individuals with respect to their rational decision making context and reference base. Even if a particular situation looks favorable for an offense to occur, there will still be a difference in the way each individual perceives the viability and the actual carrying out of the criminal act. The ramifications of individual diversity are that preventive strategies would seem to require individually tailored deterrence policies— a goal which is by all means impossible. Thus, despite Clarke and Cornish's (1985) enthusiasm, thinking of criminal behavior in terms of rational decision points is important in understanding individual offenses, but may not prove to be very useful in terms of formulating viable policies to prevent crime. Currently, the cognitive decision making approach appears to need more research and specificity to answer some very basic questions about the specialization of criminality.

SUMMARY

This chapter has attempted to distinguish yet another area in the study of the psychology of crime. Granted, it is a fledgling area of study regarding criminal activity, but the importance of the questions cognitive theorists are asking assures its survival as a focus of study in the psychology of crime. The key contribution of cognitive psychology is the interactive focus of internal states with situational factors. Cognitive psychology may help explain someday the differences between individuals who share basically the same social backgrounds, but act so differently in similar situations.

We began this chapter by highlighting the differences that separate a cognitive approach from psychoanalytical, trait, and behaviorist approaches. After further reflection, however, a more accurate way of thinking about cognitive theory may be as a merger of all these different theoretical paradigms into a working theory of the individual in a social environment. Certainly cognitive theory borrows a little from psychoanalysis in the form of needs; a little from trait theory in the form of attributes like intelligence, impulsiveness, and empathy; a little from behaviorism with respect to the environment as stimulus- response. Borrowing from such a diverse number of theoretical camps makes cognitive theory a rather robust approach to studying individual criminal behavior.

This chapter on cognitive perspectives in the study of crime has provided an overview of some of the literature in three general areas. The first area dealt with elements of the thinking process (e.g., intelligence and impulsiveness) that correlated with criminal activity. The second area focused on criminal psychology research regarding self-concept and the thinking process, or how one's self-concept influences one's choice in committing criminal acts. The last focus of this chapter concerned criminal decision making. This section looked at research dealing with the process by which individuals contemplate and make decisions to actually carry out a criminal act.

The biggest drawback to cognitive approaches is their inability to generalize beyond very small groups of individuals. Cognitive psychology is basically the study of an individual's personal and background variables and their interaction with different situational contexts. Each individual takes to a particular situation a bundle of life experiences and reference points which provide a hodgepodge of possible courses of action. The goal of the cognitive theorist studying crime has been to better understand the most important life experiences and reference points from which criminal decisions are made.

Six

Existential and Phenomenological Perspectives

UNFORTUNATELY, the application of existential and phenomenological perspectives to the study of crime has been rare. This may be due to the apparent incompatibility of these perspectives with positivistic approaches. Existential and phenomenological perspectives avoid "psychologizing" (reducing the totality of the individual to mere psychological variables) and opt for a more holistic approach. These perspectives are more humanistic and concern themselves with analyzing levels of consciousness, individual strivings, choices and immediate experiences, then attempting to formulate broad theoretical perspectives of social life. Crime is often explained with some reference to an ontology of human striving, a theory about existence, or explanation for why individuals construct the meanings, purposes and cultures which define them.

Existential and phenomenological perspectives are also a reaction to pure psychoanalytic, behavioristic, and trait approaches in the study of human behavior. Existentialists and phenomenologists differ from psychoanalysts in their assumption about the amount of freedom individuals have over their lives. Existentialists and phenomenologists believe individuals possess volition (or will), hence the ability to choose and create themselves. Psychoanalytic theory suggests that the individual possesses little freedom, due to the influence of unconscious forces (i.e., primal drives and repressed desires).

Trait theorists also believe individuals possess limited freedom, because particular traits determine personality. Existentialists and phenomenologists, on the other hand, view individual behavior as much less determined by internal psychological forces, traits, or external stimuli (as the behaviorists do). They maintain a more holistic perspective, acknowledging that humans operate from many levels of consciousness and continuously create and define their world. This is not to say that existentialists and phenomenologists denounce the importance of social environment in shaping the context of individual choices. Rather, they would claim, human action results from the interaction of internal and external processes.

Existential and phenomenological perspectives are similar to the cognitive perspective in their desire to explain crime in terms of the interaction between internal and situational factors. The basic differences between them, however, are their methodologies (positivism versus phenomenology — the study of forms of consciousness and immediate experiences) and their starting points (information processing versus ontological striving — the quest to give meaning to one's existence). Cognitive theory is more atomistic in its approach to understanding personality, whereas existential and phenomenological theories are more holistic.

In this section, we will explore two theoretical perspectives describing criminal activity as a process of existential striving and phenomenological experiences. The first theoretical perspective we will explore stems from the work of S. Giora Shoham (1979) and the second perspective comes from the existential and phenomenological work of Jack Katz (1988). Before inquiring into these perspectives, a brief overview of existential and phenomenological psychological perspectives is provided for necessary historical and substantive background.

The Origins of Existential Psychology

Existential approaches to psychology grew out of a concern for understanding individuals as totalities in relation with their environments.

EXISTENTIAL PERSPECTIVES

Existentialism deals with the unique quality of human beings to reflect back upon themselves. "Humans are capable of 'standing out of' or 'extending beyond' themselves through self-consciousness, self-reflection, transcendence through supra-individual values, creativity, work, and in love and friendship" (Massey, 1981:439). This ability to move outside ourselves is where the concept of human freedom originates. Because humans are self-reflective, they can change their conditions by making choices. The ability, however, to make choices, create, and define ourselves is always restricted or confined by our social environment. For an existentialist, every choice entails responsibility and consequences.

Existential psychology finds its origins in the work of a group of philosophers who have been labeled existentialists largely because they revolted "against traditional philosophy" (Kaufmann, 1975:11). Some of the individual philosophers most often equated with the existential avantgarde are Kierkegaard (1813-1855), Nietzsche (1844-1900), Dostoevsky (1821-1881), Heidegger (1889-1976), Sartre (1905-1980), and Buber (1878-1965).

The existential motif expounded by Kierkegaard (1980) dealt with the anxiety and dread that accompanies an awareness of our inevitable mortality. Nietzsche (1956, 1966) challenged the entire Western tradition by first perceiving human beings as creatures of will rather than creatures of reason. Dostoevsky (1957, 1961) pushed the concept of human consciousness to it limits by noting that we can, with full self-awareness, act against our own self-interest.

Based on the premises of these philosophers' perspectives on the human condition, existential personality theorists "have attempted to uncover the fundamental characteristics of persons as they use their capacities for freedom and responsibility to negotiate authentic existences for themselves, within their own particular circumstances" (Massey, 1981:439). Some popular existential psychologists include Ludwig Binswanger (1881-1966), Victor Frankl, and Rollo May.

Binswanger, who was heavily influenced by German philosopher Martin Heidegger, perceived existential analysis as a perspective which examines "human existence prior to any split into subject and object" (Massey, 1981:440). Binswanger used the term *Dasien* to describe the basis of human existence. *Dasien* translates into English as "being-in-the-world" (Massey, 1981:441). For Binswanger, Dasien means that humans are born without any choice into a historical period over which they have no control. Accordingly, human freedom, choice and responsibility are shaped by a historical context. Each person is responsible for creating their own "world design" within their historical situation (Massey, 1981:440-441). The goal of human existence is to achieve an authentic, autonomous self.

Victor Frankl, who spent three years of his life in a German concentration camp during World War II, experienced and witnessed existential striving first hand. The human need to give meaning and purpose to a situation has never been more apparent than in the Nazi concentration camps. Frankl believed even in the most depraved conditions that one human freedom always remained, "to choose one's attitude in any given set of circumstances, to choose one's way" (1963:104). Frankl's concerns have been more closely associated with existential therapy than personality theory (see Corey, 1991). Frankl held love to be the most important and cherished guide to human striving.

Rollo May (1969) has written a rather influential book titled *Love and Will,* which confronts the crisis of love in modern society. In this book, May describes modern society as going through a transitional stage marked by anomie (normlessness), emptiness, and meaninglessness. His book is an attempt to analyze and diagnose the source of this alienation and meaninglessness and to offer sober solutions to this dilemma.

For May (1969), the defining characteristic of individuals is their ability to step outside themselves. This implies that individuals also have the ability to choose their identities. Of course, with choice comes responsibility and anxiety. However, building a self based on chosen ideals and goals can bring the individual self-empowerment and a great sense of joy (Massey, 1981).

The key issues for existential psychologists have been exploring individuals' experiences with respect to human freedom, responsibility, will and power. Existential psychologists have attempted to study the characteristics with which individuals deal with freedom, choice, and responsibility in shaping their identities as individuals. In short, existential psychology explores the ways in which individuals use their freedom and choices to create meaning in their lives.

The methodological tools of existential psychology have their origins in the philosophical and methodological perspectives of phenomenology. Phenomenological psychology is steeped in the philosophical view of

Edmund Husserl (1859-1938). Husserl (1975) felt that phenomenology should set its sights on getting back "to the things themselves." Husserl characterized phenomenology as an inquiry into various forms of human experiences and levels of consciousness. He believed that philosophy should aim at providing introspective descriptions of individuals' conscious inner worlds, descriptions that focus on forms of consciousness and experience such as religion, aesthetics, sensuality, and morality. In short, Husserl (1975) argued for a descriptive philosophy of the inner experiences of everyday human life.

Taken together, existential and phenomenological perspectives form a unique focus for studying individual criminal behavior. Existentialism can be understood as a belief that existence precedes essence (Sartre, 1968), that human beings as having no essential nature other than the latent power of choice, which is then used to create meaning and self-definition. Existentialism is a perspective on the human condition and human existence (i.e., an ontology). This perspective assumes the absence of an essential human nature and purpose which confronts individuals when they become aware of it, with strong feelings of alienation, anxiety, and a fear of mortality. Individuals strive to overcome this condition by creating a sense of meaning and worth.

In conjunction with existentialism, phenomenology is a unique philosophical view and methodological strategy for studying the subjective inner states of human beings. Most of the inner states studied by phenomenologists are existential in nature; in other words, phenomenologists study the individual as individual.

With this as an overview to existential and phenomenological orientations in psychology, we will now turn to two applications of these perspectives in the study of crime. The first application we will embark on is the personality theory of S. Giora Shoham. Shoham's work is unique in its interdisciplinary nature and depth of analysis. Shoham's (1979) personality theory is grounded in existential themes of human striving, separation, and self-awareness. However, note that Shoham's (1979) personality theory is more than just an existential and a phenomenological analysis; it also implicitly incorporates several different psychological perspectives, including psychoanalysis, trait, social learning and cognitive theories. Although Shoham's theory is quite versatile, we have placed it in this section because of its ultimate concern with human striving, meaning, and experience.

S. Giora Shoham: Mytho-Empiricism and Ontology

One of the most powerful tools available to the social psychologist, if not misused, is historical analysis. There are several ways to utilize history, and Shoham draws on many of them. However, he anchors his theory in one particular historical approach which he labels mytho-empiricism (Shoham, 1983a:38). This is the study of cultural myths looking for what they can reveal about human striving and existence. Through historical analysis and cross cultural comparison, Shoham has built his theory around the most universal mythical projections. The myth, for Shoham, serves as an empirical anchor which he perceives as a projection of the most intimate knowledge of the human condition.

Shoham offers a provocative analysis of how myths serve as personal projections of the catastrophe of birth. Borrowing from Eliade's analysis of myths, Shoham shares the assumption that underlying each culture are myths which constitute its "origins, beginnings and births" (Eliade in Shoham, 1979:20). For both Eliade and Shoham, the myth is inextricably linked with ontology. Therefore, "it speaks only of realities, of what really happened, of what was fully manifested" (Eliade in Shoham, 1979:20). In addition, drawing from Jung, Shoham (1979:20) contends,

> ...some myths are accounts of a personal reality; a projection onto the cosmos of one's earliest life experiences. Once impressed on the newborn, the experience of birth is never irretrievably lost but may find expression through myths of genesis and creation.

Shoham's personality theory, then, is anchored in some of the universal themes discerned through an interdisciplinary analysis of the tales of creation and genesis found in mythologies, religious orthodoxies, literary and oral narratives.

The predominant motif in Shoham's theoretical perspective is that birth is a cosmic disaster associated with the creation of evil. For example, most Christian doctrines tend to proclaim that humans are born into this world with original sin, which must be expunged by the ritual of baptism. Shoham also draws from Buddhism, the Kabbala, Hinduism, and a host of other spiritual explanations which all address the universal fall from grace. Shoham contends that "[t]he biblical account of Original Sin and the Fall from Grace has its parallels in most of the world religions. It has its roots in folklore and is a truth myth in its archetypal significance as a projection of personal history" (Shoham, 1979:92).

The universal fall has been interpreted from many perspectives, always ending in the separation of the individual from all things. In the Buddhist tradition the unity of all things may be discerned in temporal existence through processes of transformation and meditative states. This, however, requires the annihilation of ego or the fusing of subject/object reality. Birth, death, and rebirth are seen as a continual process of achieving perfection with the ultimate aim being Nirvana. Nirvana is the highest good wherein full enlightenment and nothingness are one. Achievement of this state "releases one from the wheel of rebirth, suffering and ignorance" (Frazier, 1970:300). There is no god or other to return to, whereas in the Christian tradition the return to grace requires an historical event (i.e., the return of God and the dissolution of the temporal world). For agnostics and some existentialists the tragedy of alienation and relativism are a secular evil.

For Shoham this process of representing birth as evil and a separation, becomes the universal foundation for philosophical and theological postulates of good and evil. In all known human societies, there is some type of good and evil dichotomy which allows for choice. Thus, Shoham argues that faith is universal. He writes:

> The belief in God and the ever-after is a narrow segment of the human encounter with transcendence. Of wider relevance is the fact that our whole conception of reality —things, flora, fauna and other human beings "out there" is of necessity based on faith. Thus we make our distinction between good and bad. This makes transcendence a vital component in the explanation...of deviance and crime (Shoham, 1979:3).

Shoham offers us a metaphysical starting point for conjecturing about deviance and links it with the bio-psychological disposition of separate human existence.

To reiterate, the creation myth is a projection of one's personal history. The cross cultural study of creation myths provides a universal theme construed as the fall from bliss, from completeness or divinity. Birth is a crisis that separates the individual from "pantheistic togetherness" (Shoham, 1979). The human being enters the world as an ontologically separated being who is aware of this crisis on various levels of consciousness.

Separation from bliss is the foundation of evil. Humans, unlike any other species, have to construct ethical and moral systems of good and evil — not only for their biological survival as a species, but also to undo the tragedy of separation — by devising accepted modes of participation to return to the longed for bliss.

Shoham and Personality Development

Shoham's theory is unequivocally a personality dynamic, where the focus is upon the individual. The theory operates from existential premises; humans are ontologically lonely beings, driven to seek one of many avenues of transcendental, ontological, or social participation. Although the focus is on the individual, cultural and social structures are important dimensions which interact with the individual's core personality dynamics. These external structures also dictate which avenues of participation will be deemed acceptable and which will be branded as deviant.

Shoham's theory operates from two diametrically opposed vectors which interact at three major focal points of personality development: birth, ego formation, and ego identity. The first vector is separation, the biological basis of behavior; that is, the birth of an individual denotes the starting point of separate forces manifested in the bio-psychological structure of being. Once a child is born it immediately ceases to be one with its universe — the mother's womb. The newborn is forced to process all ensuing stimuli as external to itself. The second vector is participation "which is structured around the quest of the individual's striving to revert to... the completeness of non-being" (Shoham et al., 1987:354). Simply put, the participation vector should be construed as a subjective yearning to undo the tragedy of bio-psychological being. The interaction of these two forces should be perceived as what makes temporal existence tolerable for some and unbearable for others.

Shoham's theoretical foundation begins with the recording of the personal and mythological catastrophe of separation at birth (i.e., the first focal point) which is antithetical to the pantheistic bliss experienced and recorded by the fetus in the womb. It is important to discern throughout Shoham's thesis that recorded deep in the human psyche is a pure form of holistic bliss, a nonconsciousness, a plenary participation experienced prior to birth. The infant's journey from the cushioned womb through the birth canal, out into a foreign world is an extremely traumatic event. The fetus, once enveloped in an all-satiating milieu, unable to distinguish itself from its surroundings, now is thrust into a world which is literally colder, harder, and brighter than that experienced in the womb. In this sense, birth is a catastrophe, a rupture which separates the infant from the wholeness experienced prior to its expulsion into a precarious world (Shoham, 1979:27-31).

From here on, the pressure of separation increases with the maturation of the child at the second focal point of personality development, ego formation. Ego formation is the point in cognitive development where the child distinguishes itself as a separate entity from objects around it through the pain and discomfort that is experienced in hunger, thirst, and the bumps and bruises experienced in the exploration of its surroundings. These temporal discomforts, accompanied "with the mother, who is often not 'good' and 'caring' but 'bad' and 'depriving'... push the newborn child to crystallize a separate entity and to depart from pantheistic togetherness with his [sic] surroundings" (Shoham et al., 1987:355). In other words, the subject/object barrier becomes the psychological equivalent of an ego barrier.

For Shoham, the personality type and concomitant attributes of the individual are anchored in the fixation of the child at one of two possible stages that occur before or after the ego's formation. Fixation is usually caused by some kind of trauma or crisis resulting from a feeling of deprivation or unsatisfactory interaction with the child's parents or surroundings: for example, the first time a parent does not respond promptly or perhaps correctly to a child's cries. The first stage is early orality wherein the subject/object dichotomy has not yet taken place. Simply put, the child maintains a holistic essence where the self and other is not yet differentiated. Shoham's theory states, "if the traumatic fixation has occurred before the generation of a separate self it results in a participant type, constantly longing to revert to early orality and to suspended animation in utero" (Shoham et al., 1987:358). By a participant type, Shoham is referring to a personality disposition. At this juncture we have a participant vector with a participant type, which we will clarify shortly.

The second stage is characterized by the child's ability to distinguish between subject and object, self and other. In this context, the child attributes deprivation to the external object. Shoham asserts, "[i]f the traumatic fixation occurs after the crystallization of the separate self, the result is a separant type, who struggles to cope with the surrounding objects and life forms" (Shoham, et al., 1987:358). To reiterate, the participant and separant types are personality dispositions both buttressed by the participant vector (i.e., the force or yearning to revert back to nothingness). The stages at which fixation occurs coupled with the participation vector determines the perceptions of self (e.g., good/bad) and perceptions of objects (e.g., good/bad).

The participant personality type is "characterized by a feeling of 'bad' me and an anxious fixation with distracting the 'good object'..."(Shoham et al. (1987:358). Because the fixation occurred when the child was unable to distinguish between subject and object, the ego formation is such that the child perceives its deprivation as a by-product of itself and not of the objects in its environment. As such, "the participant vector of the participant type will seek to annul the temporal self in order to achieve the longed for participation" (Shoham et al., 1987:358). Participants wish to be consumed by their environments. Some characteristics of the participant personality type are passiveness and introversion.

In contrast, the separant personality type perceives the object as bad and the self as good, because fixation took place after the subject/object distinction had been made. Thus, "the participant vector of the separant personality type will seek to merge — realistically or symbolically — the object within the personality" (Shoham et al., 1987:359). In other words, the separant seeks to consume the object, thus incorporating it into "good" self. Characteristics of the separant type are activeness and extroversion.

Shoham's personality types should not be understood as motivational forces to deviance. Rather, they should be construed as psychological dispositions which interact with various social forces (e.g., family, school, religion, culture, society etc.). Both personality types may be expressed in acceptable and deviant modes of participation within the various dimensions (e.g., transcendental, ontological, and social). The key issue is that the subject/object dilemma is perceived as a separating force that must be mitigated, conquered, or obliterated. Shoham has posited numerous scenarios for his personality types in interaction with parents, family, and different cultural emphases (i.e., West and East), of which a complete analysis is well beyond the scope of this chapter (see Shoham, 1979, 1983a, 1983b, 1985, 1987).

For our purpose there are three important themes that need recapitulation. First, ego formation is a separation caused by bio-psychological development. Second, fixation occurring either before or after ego formation determines a subject/object relationship entailing either good or bad perceptions of self and good or bad perceptions of objects. Finally, regardless of the personality type, the individual is driven to obliterate the subject/object barrier in the temporal world. This is a lifelong quest.

The separation pressures continue with the final stage of personality development, ego identity. This stage is affected by various socializing agencies, which exert the pressures of adult responsibilities (e.g., family expectations, school, and conventional institutions). To put it in a cross-cultural context, this stage might be conceived of as the rite of passage. This stage firmly entrenches the separation effect by reinforcing the ontologically lonely individual. Responsibility and independence become the main values of adult life.

Participation is a universal, subjective yearning for that which is anchored in faint memories prior to birth. Separating forces result from the bio-psychological structure of cognition and the demands of temporal existence. From here on, the ego makes a relentless effort to reverse this tragedy of separation, but the effort is hopeless. As such:

> Achievement of the longed for participation is attempted by negating one of the three main foci of separation. These attempts may be either deviant or institutionalized: mystics yearn to achieve perfect participation by the reversal of birth and the obliteration of self... crime and social deviation can be ways of neutralizing the social stage of normative separation. Institutionalized means include... creativity [which] may bridge the gap between subject and object; love may temporarily melt the ontological partition between human beings; and revelations may momentarily expose the individual to the wholeness of nothingness (Shoham et al., 1987:356).

Separate focal points are embedded in adult cognition and are never irretrievably lost. That is, religious participation might be interpreted as negation of birth and a longing to return to unity. The negation of the subject/object barrier may be expressed by merging oneself in the conventional avenues of social participation (e.g., an ethnic affiliation, church membership, political parties, etc.) or by obliteration of the 'bad' self through narcotics, suicide, and modes of mystical participation aimed at asceticism (Shoham, 1979:13). The strength of Shoham's ontology is the diversity of its application to deviance.

Transcendental Dimensions of Deviance

The transcendental aspects of normative and deviant behavior are negations of the separation effect encountered in the tragedy of birth. Therefore, transcendental projects are an attempt to overcome or compensate for the first focal point of the separation crisis, birth. The best way to make the transcendental aspect of deviance discernible is to counterpose with it conceptions of normative modes of religious participation. At this focal point it is imperative to understand the notion of a lost paradise upon the advent of birth. Comprising both the deviant and normative individual are the same yearnings, needs, and desires to reverse the tragedy of separate existence. One way this attempt is made is through different modes of religious participation.

Normative modes of religious participation are meant to relinquish the suffering of temporal life. They are a way of obliterating oneself through fusion with transcendental ultimates (e.g., God). For example, the practice of communion for Christians, the search for Nirvana in Buddhism, and Brahman in Hinduism are all ritualistic and symbolic attempts to achieve fusion with universal wholeness. Religions are, as Shoham suggests:

> ...a colossal proof for the intense longing of humans to cease to be what they are, to surrender the burden of existence they did not ask for, to sever all the stages that made this absurd and painful drudgery, to obliterate consciousness, to go back to the pantheistic togetherness of infancy, to revert to the parental blissful floating, back to the womb (1979:46).

What distinguishes the normative form of participation from the deviant is deference to the laws. In short, the normative mode of transcendental participation is institutionalized, and guided by the mandates of proper ritualism and membership.

The transcendental deviant mode of participation is through inversion, or as Shoham (1979) asserts, "beatitude through sin." Deviance on this plane constitutes decisive conscious acts aimed at inverting everything commonly assumed to be righteous and sacred in life. It is the desire to reverse the tragedy of birth, an attempt to annihilate individuality and the complete negation of evil. The transcendental deviant seeks destruction of good and evil rooted in individuality in order to achieve the longed for unity. Only through destruction of temporal life can the transcendental

EXISTENTIAL PERSPECTIVES 123

deviant find unity through symbolic nonbeing. To illustrate this point, take for example this statement by Jacob Frank — an 18th century self-proclaimed Jewish messiah — to his followers:

> I did not come into this world to lift you up but rather to cast you down to the bottom of the abyss... The descent into the abyss requires not only the rejection of all religions and conventions, but also the commission of strange acts and this in turn demands the voluntary abasement of one's own sense of self, so that libertinism and the achievement of the state of utter shamelessness leads to a state in which all laws and religion are annihilated (Frank in Shoham, 1979:2).

The whole point of the transcendental deviant is to descend into the abyss in order to ascend into the heavens (Shoham, 1979:55-82).

Self-proclaimed deviant messiahs are nothing new to the 20th century as exemplified by Jim Jones, Charles Manson, and David Koresh. Shoham's concept of the transcendental deviant offers insight into the recent increase of satanic worship and interest in the occult.

Ontological Dimensions of Deviance

The participation vector discussed earlier suggests that individuals seek union to overcome the anxiety of separation. The ontological dimensions of deviance are best understood as those modes of participation meant to relinquish the subject/object barrier. Because Shoham posits birth and ego formation as the major separation foci, the modes of participation aimed at negating these pressures overlap to some degree. For instance, Buddhism practices both transcendence and subject/object unity by attempting to overcome desires which impede the goal of higher consciousness. For the most part, however, the subject/object problem remains a temporal quest.

The ontological dimensions of crime are those acts which are demarcated by deviant labels, not those which constitute an "evil" within themselves. In short, the yearning for participation is universal, but its particular form is either normal or deviant depending on cultural construction. Cultural norms, then, may be relative, but human interaction within a culture has yearning for participation as a universally common denominator. One way to explain ontological dimensions of crime is to contrast them with normative avenues of participation.

Normative paths to ontological participation are illusory attempts to merge oneself with objects, knowledge, and/or truth by mastery over them or submission to them. These attempts are illusory because neither objects, knowledge, nor truth have any objective reality. A normative emphasis on this focal point means fusing oneself with objects or causes to the point of losing one's identity. For example, patriotism and political causes tend to serve this purpose well for many individuals. People die in battle for their country not as separate individuals, but as part of a bigger cause (e.g., freedom, democracy). As Snow points out, "[w]hen you think of the long and gloomy history of man, you will find more hideous crime have been committed in the name of obedience than in the name of rebellion" (in Bandura, 1986:216).

The deviant ontological correlate is existential introspection. As one example of ontological deviance, let us take the use of illegal narcotics, a major political and social concern in the last few years. Drug use and abuse have been phenomena throughout most of human history and have presented themselves in rather diverse ways (Kavaler, 1965). People have used narcotics to gain relief from physical ailments, to achieve mystical unity in religious ritual (still a common practice among certain Native American tribes), and for recreation. We are concerned in this analysis with recreational use, rationalized by the common cliche, "I am unwinding," and sometimes with the religious motivation of seeking unity.

While gravitating toward narcotics can be a learned process, it is difficult to deny that certain narcotics serve some function specific to an individual's psychological needs. Certain narcotics, (e.g., marijuana, peyote, and LSD) distort perceptions of time and space, and offer the user feelings of euphoria. A common accusation made against users of illegal narcotics is that they are escapists. In the U.S., this kind of escapism goes against a deeply ingrained Puritan work ethic. This theme has been expounded by innumerable advertising campaigns (e.g., "say no to drugs, and yes to a whole lot more").

Explanations for why individuals use narcotics tend to ignore existential dimensions of the issue and the fact that narcotic use is an all-pervasive phenomenon. It is not confined to either smart or simple people; it is not the preference of one subculture over another; and it does not appear to be the result of a particular psychological attribute or trait that can be classified in any one specific category. Rather it might be more helpful to view the use of illegal narcotics as a way of alleviating separation pressures both internal and external. Drug use can be construed as an escape route back to a yearned for sense of wholeness. Put another way, narcotics are a way to relieve the tension of what some individuals feel is an unbearable, lonely reality.

The high level of narcotics consumption (this includes alcohol) in Western culture attests to the fact that escapism has much deeper implications than those readily given by current theories of deviance. Shoham's personality dynamic provides a view of this phenomenon as a problem of living partly internally and partly externally (i.e., a society with limited modes of participation). Our society emphasizes individuality as a positive attribute. Because, according to Shoham (1979), this attribute is the antithesis of what humans really yearn for, it is no wonder that drug use and suicides are so frequent in American culture.

Suicide in this framework can also be conceived of as the ultimate attempt to obliterate subject/object reality, where the finality of the consequences speak for themselves. On this level of introspection, the only real question may be, as Camus so bluntly put it, "whether or not to commit suicide" (1961:3). Existential introspection within this paradigm may be interpreted as the ultimate realization of a separate condition. All attempts to cope with this realization become futile, and in the end, life becomes meaningless.

In sum, the ontological and transcendental dimensions of deviance are apparent in some criminal striving. With the aid of Shoham's ontology and personality dynamic, we are able to make sense out of phenomena not easily accounted for in conventional psychological theories of crime.

Shoham's Social Dimension of Deviance

Both the ontological and transcendental modes of deviance should be construed as parts of the human psyche that operate on intuition and mysticism, and perceive time and space as boundless. The other side of the psyche is the rational ordering of time, space and causality. It is quite difficult to deny both of these dimensions in human beings, and it is equally difficult to deny that they often function in conflict. For example, political leaders often make "rational" decisions to go to war, yet they ask God to bless their cause. There is nothing so poignant as the rational human lamenting to the gods when help is needed or when all else fails. The focus of this section is to highlight the social dimension of deviance, which reflects the rational ordering of the psyche.

For Shoham, the first need of any individual is biological survival (e.g., food and nourishment 1979:177) He suggests that the psychological need for attachment comes much later on and is "the child's last defense against total separation after the severance from the umbilical cord and expulsion from the pantheistic bliss of early orality" (1979:177). Attachment to the family becomes the central socializing agent and the beginning of social participation. Later on the family becomes sublimated by other modes of participation found in work institutions, churches, social groups, etc.

Deviant participation on the social level is the negation of the third focal point, ego identity. Responsibilities, norms, and laws are major separative pressures on both the deviant and normal individual. Conformity depends on the serving of physical and emotional ties to childhood and parent. Shoham (1979:180-183) asserts:

> ...the extinction of emotional dependence is one of the major aims of "normal" socialization... The burdens of responsibility inherent in social separation are imposed on the child through its developing a conscience and the mechanism of guilt and shame. These in turn are at the basis of the processes of social control that aim at keeping the individual within the normative pigeon-hole.

Deviance in this light is a rejection of these normative pressures and is interpreted psychologically as a yearning to return to the irresponsibilities of childhood and the fold of the family. However, the return to the family and to a life of irresponsibility is obviously impossible; it is a lost paradise. The individual who is not ready to join the ranks of society finds other ways to fulfill her/his desires (e.g., delinquent subcultures and gangs).

Shoham does not provide just one explanation for why some people are more prone to delinquent rather than normative modes of participation. Certain psychological dispositions stemming from ego formation, accompanied by interaction with parents, family and other socializing agencies determine various normative and deviant modes of participation. Shoham and Rahav (1982) have written extensively on the effects of labeling, which they suggest is a plausible explanation for recidivism and eventually more serious criminal patterns.

In sum, Shoham's ontology and personality dynamic provide a perspective as to why individuals are driven to the social world, mainly because it is the last option available for easing the sense of separation that confronts them. The social world provides avenues for social participation, either normative or deviant, that allow individuals a point of refuge. According to Shoham, whether the individual chooses a normative or deviant mode of participation is of secondary concern. The primary need is to relieve the tensions of the unbearable ontological reality of separation.

Jack Katz: Crime as Seduction

Jack Katz's *Seductions of Crime: Moral and Sensual Attractions in Doing Evil* (1988), is an excellent combination of both existential and phenomenological approaches to the study of crime. As noted earlier, existential and phenomenological approaches tend to shy away from psychologizing (i.e., atomizing attributes of individual behavior) and Katz's book is no exception. Katz (1988) uses inductive ethnographic techniques to get at the heart of lived social experiences of crime. Simply put, he analyzes the motivations, emotions, and projects of individuals who commit crime. After analyzing these dimensions of the individual, he formulates conceptual theoretical models which provide an explanation of the purpose and meaning of criminal activity. Katz seeks to answer the question, "what are people trying to do when they commit a crime?" (1988:9).

A unique dimension of Katz's *Seductions of Crime* (1988) is his distinction between background and foreground factors. By background factors, Katz (1988) means those psychological variables like impulsiveness, self control, intelligence; or sociological variables such as broken homes, unemployment; or social class. Each type of variable has held the attention of criminologists at the expense of phenomenological experiences of crime. Katz (1988) argues that we have ignored the "seductive qualities of crime", the things that make crime sensual, morally transcendent, emotional, and perhaps spiritual. Katz is most interested in exploring the details of the criminal experience while committing a crime; these details are what he means by foreground factors.

By focusing on the phenomenological experiences of criminality, Katz (1988) seriously challenges behavioristic and utilitarian motives for criminality. For Katz, the conventional belief that all crime is a calculated endeavor aimed at obtaining pleasurable rewards (see Walters and White, 1989; Wilson and Herrnstein, 1985; Gottfredson and Hirschi, 1990) seems to negate the fact that most crime is done with little premeditation. Accordingly, Katz perceives many spontaneous crimes as involving individuals who attempt to establish a transcendent status (i.e., a tough guy or a street elite). He states, "one must consider the essential project as transcending the modern moral injunction to adjust the public self sensitively to situationally contingent expectation" (Katz, 1988:81). According to Katz, pleasure is not the motive for crime, but an epiphenomenon of the construction process of self. The creation of self identity is the primary motive, pleasure merely a derivative of obtaining the identity sought.

Katz's concerns, then, lie in detailing the lived experience of the criminal. He notes, "as unattractive morally as crime may be, we must appreciate that there is genuine experiential creativity in it as well" (Katz, 1988:8). For each particular crime, Katz proposes:

> a different set of individually necessary and jointly sufficient conditions, each set containing (1) a path of action —distinctive practical requirements for successfully committing the crime, (2) a line of interpretation —unique ways of understanding how one is and will be seen by others, and (3) an emotional process —seductions and compulsions that have special dynamics (1988:9).

Using individual case analyses of offenders and offenses ranging from murder to vandalism, Katz's (1988) project is to understand the feelings, emotions and moral justifications that comprise criminal actions.

Providing the foundation for Katz's phenomenological concerns is his ontology of human striving; at the core of Katz's portrayal of the deviant individual is the assumption that criminals attempt to maintain, through their criminal actions, a sense of meaning and moral worth. In essence, criminals attempt to transcend moral existence, either by bolstering or maintaining self worth. In Chapter One, entitled "Righteous Slaughter", Katz (1988) provides an analysis of several different murder cases which portray offenders defending what they believe to be the "Good." He states: "I arrive at a definition of the problem to be explained as 'righteously enraged slaughter,' or an impassioned attack through which the assailant's attempts to embody in his victim marks that will eternally attest to the assailant's embrace of a primordial Good" (Katz, 1988:18). Katz goes on to identify three stages in which the righteous slaughter takes place.

The following is an illustration of the analytical style of Katz's phenomenological approach to a typical homicide — one not committed with premeditation. Katz (1988:18-19) suggests:

1. The would-be killer must interpret the scene and the behavior of the victim in a particular way. He must understand not only that the victim is attacking what he, the killer, regards as an eternal human value, but that the situation requires a last stand in defense of his basic worth.

2. The would-be killer must undergo a particular emotional process. He must transform what he initially senses as an eternally humiliating situation into a rage. In rage, the killer can blind himself to his future, forging a momentary sense of eternal unity with the Good.

3. The would-be killer must successfully organize his behavior to maintain the required perspective and emotional posture while implementing a particular project. The project is the honoring of the offense that he suffered through a marking violently drawn into the body of the victim. Death may or may not result, but when it does, it comes as a sacrificial slaughter.

All told, Katz sees some homicidal offenders' actions as the pursuit of a moral conviction (e.g., humiliation, righteousness, or vengeance), which evolves into rage. While committing the murder, these offenders believe they are transcending everyday moral existence in defense of goodness, which ultimately boils down to their sense of self.

Katz's (1988) entire book is a rich phenomenological analysis of different forms of criminality (e.g., from homicide to vandalism) explained in relation to moral transcendence. One of the most commendable attributes of the book is its attempt to get inside criminals' heads to understand their feelings and their reasoning. This contribution is monumental in that it requires a fundamental re-examination of what may be an over emphasis in the sociology and psychology of crime on background factors. Simply put, not all people who come from economically deprived conditions or rate high on impulsiveness scales commit crime. This suggests that some people, criminals, find something unique, something seductively alluring, about their victims or objects of desire. The fact that many criminal acts happen without premeditation also suggests that criminal interactions evolve within a complicated interpersonal situation, whether it be with another individual or with an object of desire. Katz has simply made us aware that by ignoring the lived experience of crime, we have left out the 'why' of criminality. Similarly situated people do not all act alike.

Katz has offered us a tactical link between aggregate data and the motivational needs of individuals.

The most important issue Katz (1988) puts before us as students of crime is ultimately epistemological. He has challenged us to look seriously at criminality as a lived, experiential, and situational context as opposed to viewing criminality as dependent upon background factors. Katz is not alone in asking us to consider the subjectivity of crime. Toch (1979, 1987), for instance, has pointed out the significance in supplementing positivism with subjective experience, and Groves and Lynch (1990) have suggested that we need to take seriously the effort to combine subjective and structural approaches if we are ever to deal with multidimensional aspects of criminality.

In sum, Katz (1988) asks us to critically reexamine our unquestioning acceptance of imputed background factors of criminality that are "invisible in [the crime's] situational manifestation" (Katz, 1988:311). Having a background of highly correlated characteristics consistent with criminality does not in the least explain why some individuals engage in criminal activity while others do not. This, according to Katz, is the relevance and significance of examining the foreground factors that lead to the actual seduction of a crime. As to what a systematic empirical theory of crime should entail, Katz suggests "one that explains at the individual level the causal process of committing a crime and that accounts at the aggregate level for recurrently documented correlations with biographical and ecological background factors" (1988:312).

Criticisms of Existential and Phenomenological Approaches

Criticisms often directed at existential and phenomenological approaches stem from their lack of scientific verification. For example, in the case of Shoham we can hardly verify empirically that myths are personal projections of the catastrophe of birth. How can we possibly measure the separation effect at birth, or how that effect is going to influence an individual's psychological disposition? As for Katz, how can we empirically verify that the primary aim of criminality is moral transcendence? How can we verify the validity of Katz's phenomenological interpretation?

The answer to these questions is that we cannot. We can never know absolutely what our motives are, or for that matter, what our nature is, because we are inextricably bound up in nature itself. That does not mean we do not make assumptions about these matters every time we begin to theorize about human behavior. What differentiates Shoham and Katz from many theorists is the candidness with which they offer us a sensible interpretation of individual striving and meaning. From empirical observations they construct a logical representation of human phenomena, whereas many of their theoretical counterparts gloss over or ignore entirely their ontological and human nature assumptions. Many perceive the ambitious pursuits of Shoham and Katz as antiscientific, but if we look deeply enough every theoretical endeavor we have studied makes assumptions about human beings of the same magnitude — the issue is how explicitly they are made.

The other major criticism of existential and phenomenological perspectives comes from the realm of policy. As with almost all the psychological theories discussed, one of their major downfalls has been their inability to effect large scale social change. This is inevitably due to the disciplinary focus of psychology, which is for the most part individually based. Nevertheless, individually based approaches do not necessarily preclude policy applications, especially when you consider that all individuals may be operating from the same ontological framework. Human striving to create a sense of meaning out of the world is endemic to both Katz's and Shoham's perspective. This striving for a sense of meaning is largely fulfilled through the interaction individuals have with their culture and with significant others. If culture and significant others are unable to fulfill this need adequately, then human suffering and social ills (such as high crime rates) are likely to occur. One recommendation, for example, from a Shohamian perspective would entail easing the separation effect imposed by culture upon individuals, by providing more ample cultural modes of participatory living (e.g., more opportunities for collaboration in work and play).

Katz's policy implications lie in his recommendation for reconciling foreground and background approaches to criminality. When we start understanding criminality as a result of human striving to overcome a sense of perceived moral inadequacy or self worth, it becomes easier to understand criminality as a product of human living, not as an enigmatic evil attribute. What follows from understanding is empathy and a policy platform that attempts to ameliorate human suffering rather than contribute to it by creating more cultural mechanisms of oppression (i.e., tougher sentencing, more police, etc.).

SUMMARY

This chapter attempted to highlight some existential and phenomenological perspectives in the study of criminality that have been ignored or glossed over in most psychology texts on the study of crime. Existential and phenomenological concerns deal with getting at the roots of criminality by seeking to explore human striving, motivation, and meaning. They ask questions about human awareness and being in this world; they deal with issues of human freedom and choice as defined by the social context into which individuals find themselves thrust.

Existential and phenomenological perspectives are imperative if we are ever to understand Charles Manson, Ted Bundy, Ivan Boesky, or for that matter, the more common criminals of this world. Why did a millionaire feel compelled to embezzle a million more? What compelled Manson to invert everything we assume to be 'normal' in our everyday worlds? What motivated Bundy to methodically stalk, torture and slaughter his fellow human beings? What compels a man or a woman to murder a spouse of twenty-five years during a superficial argument?

We examined the work of S. Giora Shoham (1979) and Jack Katz (1988) in order to provide some insight into these dimensions of deviance and experiential aspects of criminality. Shoham's (1979) work contributes to our understanding of crime as a result of ontological and transcendental human striving. Katz's (1988) work provides a unique methodological perspective for examining the importance of human striving and moral transcendence. Taken together, both theorists provide unique theoretical and tactical perspectives which contribute immensely to our understanding of criminality.

Existential and phenomenological perspectives, however, are not without their problems. One of these is their inability to accommodate the strict mandates of scientific inquiry. It is very difficult to operationalize concepts such as moral transcendence or ontological striving, which are considered by some to be mystical concepts, incapable of being operationalized for adequate scientific testing. Consequently, imprecise concepts and the individual dimension of existential and phenomenological approaches make difficult development of broad-based policy strategies. On the other hand, existential and phenomenological perspectives may be more representative of the social world, especially in their propensity to confront human ambiguity as a natural condition of our "reality."

Seven

New Directions for the Psychology of Crime: Transpersonal Psychology, Feminisim and Peacemaking

INCLUDING THIS chapter in a text of this nature may be considered heretical by some; however, we feel it is necessary to provide a well-rounded representation of important issues in the psychology of crime. The contents of this chapter border on a complete epistemological shift. By epistemological shift, we mean that this chapter explores entirely new ways of perceiving, knowing, thinking, and framing questions, when compared with the traditional psychological perspectives we have explored thus far. Transpersonal psychology emerged in the 1960s as a general reaction to the predominant schools of psychoanalysis, behaviorism and humanistic psychology (Walsh and Vaughan, 1980a). Transpersonal psychologists see psychoanalysis and behaviorism as "limited... in adopting a reductionistic approach to human nature, and in ignoring certain areas, concerns, and data relevant to a full study of human nature, such as values, will, consciousness, and seeking for self actualization and self transcendence" (Walsh and Vaughan, 1980a:18-19).

One of the primary goals of transpersonal psychology is to expand the area of psychological study to take into consideration issues of health and well-being. These are not areas with which criminologists have been generally concerned. Criminal psychologists specifically and criminologists in general have treated crime as a pathology that needs to be diagnosed, controlled, and if possible eradicated. However, in their eagerness to flush out and destroy crime that already exists, criminologists have excluded from their examination strategies for health and well-being conducive to creating a crime-free environment.

Humanistic psychology is an attempt to expand the parameters of psychological analysis from pathology to issues of health and well-being. Its focus is on the whole of being and experience, which differs significantly from the general tendency of psychoanalysis and behaviorism to atomize and compartmentalize aspects of individual experience and personality. Humanistic models explore the potential for self-actualization in individuals, groups and organizations. The preceding chapter on existentialism and phenomenology embodies key aspects of humanistic psychology.

Humanistic psychology differs from transpersonal psychology in one significant way. Humanistic psychology is grounded in ego centered experiences, whereas transpersonal psychology is immersed in exploring realms of consciousness which transcend ego boundaries. Abraham Maslow, an early advocate of humanistic psychology, refers to transpersonal psychology as the fourth psychology, focusing upon experiences outside of the ego level (Walsh and Vaughan, 1980).

Transpersonal psychology, then, is not only concerned with individual personality, "because personality is considered only one aspect of our psychological nature; rather it is an inquiry into the essential nature of being" (Walsh and Vaughan, 1980a:16). Transpersonal psychology is an attempt to move beyond basic ego level functioning, description and interpretation. It inquires into many realms of knowledge, synthesizing ancient wisdom, empiricism, rationalism and spiritualism (Martin, 1993). Martin (1993), in an effort to bring transpersonal psychology to the attention of criminologists, describes this melding of ways of knowing as "a useful guide for criminology" (1993).

The two areas in current criminological research that have parallel concerns with a transpersonal psychology perspective, but require some necessary qualifications, are feminism and peacemaking. Feminism has its own epistemological framework and certainly should not be placed under any theoretical rubric other than its own. The purpose of exploring feminist criminology in this chapter is to draw some analogies between feminist concerns and the transpersonal psychological perspective. Reducing feminism, however, to any perspective other than its own would be a gross injustice to feminist scholars. Our intention here is to explore feminist criticisms that suggest our current mode of doing criminology is destructive to both women and men. We will look at feminists' recommendations for attenuating the violence of criminology by focusing upon their suggestions for creating psychological health and well-being through the restructuring of social, psychological, political and economic relationships.

The peacemaking perspective also has its own epistemological domain and should not be construed as a sub-genre of any specific social science rubric. The purpose of exploring peacemaking concepts is to draw some analogies between peacemaking concerns and the transpersonal perspective. We shall also look at the peacemaking perspective's criticisms and suggested solutions for creating a social and psychological milieu more conducive to health and well-being.

Before exploring these areas of study, however, we need a more thorough presentation of transpersonal psychological concepts. Accordingly, this chapter will lay a foundation for a transpersonal perspective in criminal psychology, then explore feminism and peacemaking and their corresponding concerns.

FOUNDATIONS OF TRANSPERSONAL PSYCHOLOGY

Transpersonal psychology is an effort to expand the parameters of normal scientific inquiry by exploring areas of human consciousness which provide avenues for individuals to overcome the self-centered, isolatory effects of ego functioning (Sunberg and Keutzer, 1984). Transpersonal psychology concentrates on areas of human consciousness that transcend isolated ego experiences to inquire into extended areas of consciousness like spiritualism, mysticism and transcendence. This psychological perspective seeks to understand the full capabilities and potential of the human organism (Sunberg and Keutzer, 1984) by acknowledging the diversity of thought and action that defines human communities (Walsh and Vaughan, 1984). In short, transpersonal psychology is an attempt to perceive individuals in their natural context, as dynamic integrative beings who undergo daily a variety of human experiences, physical, psychological, sociological, and spiritual.

This attempt at integrative understanding makes the transpersonal perspective anti-reductionistic (Martin, 1993). It does not necessarily confine itself to the positivistic tenets of testable hypotheses, cogent operationalization, and the goals of experimental control and predictive understanding. Rather, transpersonal psychology seeks to expand our ways of knowing by not excluding relevant human phenomena from our study of human life. Traditionally, the goal of most psychology has been to reduce everything down to its simplest form, then exclude what does not fit the particular model at hand.

The transpersonal perspective should not be construed as anti-science, but as an attempt to "expand our views of science, or more specifically, expand our approach to knowing (i.e., to create a more inclusive paradigm)" (Martin, 1993). Transpersonal psychology perceives a need to go beyond empiricism and rationalism, the foundations of Western thought, precisely because the whole of human experience transcends these epistemological domains. For the transpersonal psychologist, a belief too firm in objective knowledge leads the theorist to exclude from the realm of inquiry a host of viable human experiences. As Ken Wilber (1979) implies, human knowledge is more or less infinite and the human ability to develop cognitively and socially is equally infinite.

Dissolving the Individual

One of the key differences between the transpersonal perspective and other psychological perspectives is its use of synthesis and holistic thinking. For instance, rather than assuming humans beings are blank slates (behaviorism) or composites of primitive impulses and desires (psychoanalysis), the transpersonal perspective accommodates all of these perspectives by realizing that individuals are "complex multidimensional whole[s]" (Walsh and Vaughan, 1980b:53). In treating human beings this way, transpersonal psychology avoids the trap that Gordon Allport trenchantly notes theorists fall into when they make totalitarian assumptions:

> By their own theories of human nature psychologists have the power of elevating or degrading that same nature. Debasing assumptions debase human beings; generous assumptions exalt them (cited in Walsh and Vaughan, 1980:8).

Making these limiting assumptions about human beings means we exclude from our focus and analysis all the times that their behavior is contrary; if we assume human nature is bad, then we fail to see when and in what way it is good. We fail to see the complexity and non-linear nature of human behavior.

Walsh and Vaughan (1980b) offer a brief outline of the four major dimensions of the transpersonal perspective which encompass the other psychological perspectives by locating them in a much wider context of human experience. The first dimension described by Walsh and Vaughan (1980b) is consciousness. By consciousness they mean "a central dimension that provides the basis and context for all experience" (Walsh and Vaughan, 1980b:54). The transpersonal perspective focuses upon the phenomenon of consciousness itself. Behaviorism, on the other hand, ignores consciousness altogether for measurement reasons, while psychoanalytical and humanistic perspectives focus more upon the structure of consciousness than upon the phenomenon itself (Walsh and Vaughan, 1980b).

According to the transpersonal perspective, there are many states of consciousness available to us, and by ignoring these states of consciousness we become prisoners in our own minds (Walsh and Vaughan, 1980b:54). Realizing that we have made ourselves prisoners of our minds is the first step to liberation. Liberation means acknowledging that "the reality we perceive reflects our own state of consciousness and we can never explore reality without at the same time exploring ourselves, both because we are, and because we create, the reality we explore" (Walsh and Vaughan, 1980b:54).

Transpersonal theorists maintain that human beings create their own realities, but they treat those realities as though they existed prior to and independently from themselves. This tendency of human beings to treat reality as absolute ignores the fact that there are many different versions of reality, and that each individual reality is only part of a much larger concept of reality. Becoming aware of our own version of reality reminds us of its relativity in relation to a world of infinite potential and possibilities.

The second dimension of transpersonal psychology identified by

Walsh and Vaughan (1980b) is the concept of conditioning. They suggest that "people are vastly more ensnared and trapped in their conditioning than they appreciate, but that freedom from this conditioning is possible" (Walsh and Vaughan, 1980b:55). Drawing from an Eastern philosophical perspective, they point out that one of the major causes of human suffering is attachment. We have attachments to particular self-images and various types of behaviors (Walsh and Vaughan, 1980b). For many, a close attachment to the status quo leads to misery and suffering. They suffer because of the pressure they impose on themselves to be "normal," to conform to the standards of a society they have reified as the only reality.

Humans build attachments not only to material objects, then, but also to ideas and social relationships. Through conditioning, many of us have become attached to the ideas and relationships which characterize the status quo of the criminal justice system. For example, how many of us would ever think of questioning the concept of state policing, prisons, or courts? How many of us ever question the premise that the solution to violence is more violence?

Unquestioned attachments to ideas and relationships lead us to continue doing things the same way, whether they work or not. They also lead us to treat people as immutable objects. For example, labeling characteristics of individuals as criminal leads us to treat these individuals as objects incapable of self-discovery and change. When, because of our own conditioning, we treat ourselves and others as unalterable objects, we negate the fact that human beings are dynamic and capable of modifying their behavior to create and meet new situations.

The third dimension associated with the transpersonal perspective is the concept of personality. Although other psychological perspectives have made personality a central role in their study, the transpersonal perspective has decentered it as a primary concern of study. Transpersonal theorists see personality "as only one aspect of being with which the individual may, but does not have to, identify" (Walsh and Vaughan, 1980b:56). Contrary to traditional perspectives advocating that we focus upon reorienting our personality to be healthy, transpersonal psychologists suggest that we should disengage from the concept of our personality as much as possible.

The final focus of study for the transpersonal perspective is the concept of identity (Walsh and Vaughan, 1980b). The concept of identity is the springboard for the transpersonal perspective to move beyond Western conceptions of the world. Identity in traditional psychological perspectives deals with the process by which an individual takes on the characteristics and feelings of others in order to become like them in some way. Transpersonal psychologists acknowledge this form of identification as external identification — its focus is directed outward.

Another form of identification that transpersonal psychologists see as more significant is the realization of internal phenomena or intrapsychic processes (Walsh and Vaughan, 1980b). They explain, "[h]ere identification is defined as the process by which something is experienced as self" (Walsh and Vaughan, 1980b:56). Walsh and Vaughan point out that most times we do not even realize this form of identification because "we are all so involved in it" (1980b:56). We never question what it is we think we are (e.g., police officer, Caucasian, heterosexual, Christian, American, etc.). This identification is usually reinforced by those around us making the intrapsychic identification process complete in context. In short, that which is not called to our attention goes unnoticed.

By not questioning who we are, our awareness fixates upon the mental content and context of our intrapsychic identification; hence, all incoming experiences are viewed from our fixed awareness. Being an American would most likely prompt you to interpret "other content, and meaning... perception, belief, motivation and behavior, all in a manner that is consistent with and reinforces this context" (Walsh and Vaughan, 1980b:57). Awareness from this position is restricted and allows for "a single self-validating perspective" (Walsh and Vaughan, 1980b:57). For example, when we as Americans go to war, we believe we are right and justified. However, the other side believes with equal conviction that they are in the right.

The transpersonal perspective, however, sees this process of intrapsychic identification as an illusion detrimental to our ability to experience the breadth of reality. As such, the transpersonal perspective looks at the implications of our ability to disidentify with these illusory intrapsychic identifications. To disidentify would loosen the hold these illusory ego identifications have over our ability to experience the world in different contexts. However, as Fromm and Suzuki point out, this is not an easy process:

> What is unconscious and what is conscious depends... on the structure of society and the patterns of feelings and thoughts it produces... The effect of society is not only to funnel fictions into our consciousness,

but also to prevent awareness of reality... Every society... determines the forms of awareness. This system works, as it were, like a socially conditioned filter; experience cannot enter awareness unless it can penetrate the filter [cited in Walsh and Vaughan, 1980b:58].

The transpersonal perspective, then, is about moving beyond the ego level form of identification and expanding our awareness to different realms of experience. It brings about the potential for human liberation, enlightenment, compassion, health and well-being. Let us examine the ramifications of this perspective for the study of crime and criminal justice policy.

Application of the Transpersonal Perspective to Crime and Policy

Although there are no purely transpersonal perspectives currently dealing with the study of crime, the potential for this perspective to shed light on particular problem areas in criminal psychology is promising. One of the most important contributions that the transpersonal perspective offers us is the knowledge that human existence is largely a creative enterprise. In other words, human beings can change unfavorable conditions by acknowledging that they exist, and how they came to exist. We create our own problems; they do not exist outside of the human mind that brought them into being.

To say crime is out of control or running rampant in our streets is to treat crime as if it were independent of our creation. Radical criminologists have been saying for a long time that we get as much crime as we deserve (Lynch and Groves, 1989). Transpersonal psychologists provide us with tools for inquiring into our resistance to change in the realm of policy.

Concepts like attachment, conditioning, and identity speak directly to many of the conceptual binds in which the criminal justice system finds itself all to often. Take, for example, the "drug war" in the United States. Drugs are often blamed for most of our street crime problems, especially violent crime. Before we accept this assumption at face value, however, we need to address the historical problem of street crime and violence in the U.S. before drugs became the convenient scapegoat. Next, if drugs are in fact the source of much of our street crime and violence, then we need to ask why the solution lies in declaring a "war" against this phenomenon rather than investigating what it is about our society that makes people feel the need to use illegal narcotics to escape their reality. The drug "war" has done little to curb the use of illegal narcotics, but has done much to escalate the amount of violence and the number of high powered weapons on our streets. The police get bigger guns, consequently the drug dealers get bigger guns, and a vicious cycle of bigger guns and more death is put into motion. Perhaps it is time to disidentify with our current Rambo-like approach and create a new way of understanding and alleviating the problem of violence.

Another problem area alluded to by Martin (1993) is with our current conception of science regarding crime and criminality. Martin has noted that "[m]ore and more individuals, across disciplines, are coming to the realization that science (at least as we have defined it) is too narrow and restrictive and that empirical/physical research is not appropriate for all things" (Martin, 1993).

Martin (1993) notes the failure of criminological theory to adequately contribute to our understanding of crime and to the failure of criminal justice policy to achieve its narrow and restricted aims. His suggestion is to treat the concept of crime and criminality as the complex phenomenon that it is, which requires removing the blinders that distort our perceptual field. Science shapes perception, and "if the scientific paradigm is limiting, then cultural/societal belief structures are limiting" (Martin, 1993). Martin's (1993) point is a good one and should not be taken too lightly in the study of crime.

If science shapes perception, then is it really objective? Many social scientists hold tenaciously to the tenets of positivism (for some very strong advocates of this position, see Gibbs, 1987; Gottfredson and Hirschi, 1987). They tend to believe that positivism is the only applicable strategy for discerning knowledge. Unfortunately, however, many of the tenets of positivism are no longer held by a majority of physical scientists. In physics, for example, Heisenberg's uncertainty principle and Schrodinger's famous cat paradox have called into question assumptions about objective observation and a deterministic universe (see for a discussion of these topics, see Capra, 1983; Gribbin, 1984; Peat, 1991; Zohar, 1990). Fritjof Capra explains (1983:87),

> In transcending the Cartesian division between mind and matter, modern physics has not only invalidated the classical ideal of an objective description of nature, but has also challenged the myth of a value free science. The patterns scientists observe in nature are

intimately connected with the patterns of their mind; with their concepts, thoughts and values... the larger paradigm within which this research is pursued will never be value free. Scientists, therefore, are responsible for their research not only intellectually but morally.

The fallacy of the objective observer requires that we become more circumspect in our use of scientific discourse and subsequent policy recommendations. Crime is not an objective phenomenon; it is, on the contrary, a very value laden subject area. A theory or an explanation of crime cannot be anything other than a description of a behavior which elicits a value judgement.

One of the most important things the transpersonal perspective has to offer us is liberation from traditional perspectives and their tenuous solutions. Transpersonal psychology provides us with the tools to examine our underlying assumptions about crime and criminal justice. Put another way, our concept of crime and criminal justice is now open for criticism, alternate conceptions, and new solutions to prevailing problems. We are not automatons carrying out some predetermined destiny. We can change, rethink and reformulate our problems of crime and criminal justice in a new light if we cast off our attachments, conditioning and egocentric identities. Human potential and creativity for solving problems is only limited by the blinders we use to restrict the wide range of experience and modes of consciousness available to us.

With this as an overview of transpersonal psychology, let us now turn to some analogous concerns in feminism and peacemaking. Both feminism and peacemaking offer us perspectives on liberation that require us to rethink our oppressive ideologies and beliefs. These perspectives seek to free us from the assumption that the world must be a violent, alienated and callous place, and instead, offer us hope for implementing values like tolerance, empathy, compassion, peacemaking, mental health, and well-being.

FEMINIST PERSPECTIVES

Historically, women's contributions to the social sciences have been neglected, and worse yet, trivialized next to those of men. Psychology and criminology are no exception to this general rule of exclusion. In addition, female centered values like tolerance and empathy, which women have maintained in spite of (or perhaps because of) a history of oppression, have generally been excluded from policy and decision making in the criminal justice system.

The majority of crime research has been done by men and has focused on men. The reason most often given for this inequity in research is that men tend to commit the most crime. Women's crime rates are rising at a faster rate than men's, specifically in areas of property crime (Bartol and Bartol, 1986; Senna and Siegel, 1993). However, overall arrest rates reveal that men do commit more crimes than women at the rate of about 4 to 1, and more violent crime at the rate of about 8 to 1 (Senna and Siegel, 1993).

One of the reasons attributed to the rising crime rates among women is the women's liberation movement (Adler, 1975). Adler (1975) contends that the rise in female criminality is a result of women becoming more assertive. She argues that women's liberation has led women to becoming more competitive and has placed them into new social positions, creating the opportunity for more criminal activity. Adler's contention, however, has been criticized for its "assumption that crime is a male activity which is therefore appealing and prestigious" (Naffine, 1987:90).

Adler has made the assumption that if women are treated like men, they will act like men. She assumes that women being treated like men is desirable, the true standard of liberation and equality. Such an assumption is highly problematic for many feminists because it reifies the patriarchal structure of society. As Naffine points out, Adler is attempting to "elevate the criminal woman to the status of the male" (1987:90). She is treating "crime as an expression of masculinity" (Naffine, 1987:91).

Other criticisms of Adler's central thesis have suggested that it misconstrues female criminality as having the same qualities as male criminality. Some argue that female criminality is not "competitive, masculine and aggressive. Nor have women achieved equality with men" (Naffine, 1987:93). According to Smart (1979), working class women have always worked outside of the home, and more often than not they have committed crimes as an attempt to compensate for severe economic strain due to low wages. Studies by Chapman (1980), Daly (1989), and Miller (1986), suggest that a majority of women offenders are usually young, single, minority women with children, who are extremely poor and often have little choice but to resort to petty crime to make ends meet. In short, Adler's liberation hypothesis has been criticized for perceiving crime as prestigious and for prompting the notion that women have lived until recently without economic stress and pressure (Naffine, 1987:99).

Explanations For Why Women Commit Less Crime

The fact that women have faced more adversity and oppression, have been devalued biologically, psychologically, sociologically, politically and economically, and yet commit far less crime than men do is an interesting phenomenon. This seems to be one of the most consistent and important empirical facts available to those studying crime. Some research has suggested that this difference between women and men is due to biological, cognitive and socialization factors.

One area of biological study has examined the difference in levels of aggression between women and men. Other than the obvious difference in size and strength between most men and women, some researchers have inferred from animal studies that male hormones, like androgen and testosterone, are more conducive to aggressive behavior (Moyer, 1973; Johnson, 1972). Thus, in conjunction with other socialization factors, physiology may account for some differences in violent behavior between women and men (Bartol and Bartol, 1986). Note, however, that attributing causes of crime to biological or physiological factors tends to create the illusion of biological determinism, which has been used throughout history to oppress women. For example, it was once believed that women had smaller brains which made them less intelligent.

The cognitive approach has been another popular approach used to account for differences in crime rates between males and females. For instance, some studies have indicated that women tend to show more empathy than men in various situations (Hoffman, 1977; Holstein, 1976), and that women often interpret aggressive situations differently than men (Frodi, Macaulay, and Thome, 1977; Barron, 1977; see for an overview of both of these topics Bartol and Bartol, 1986). In addition to these general findings is the issue of difference in moral reasoning talked about by the studies of Belenky et al. (1986), Gilligan (1982) and Morash (1983).

There is much dispute over whether these differences are due to socialization or innate predispositions. For instance, Eisenberg and Lennon (1983) suggest there is little empirical support for claiming that these differences are caused by predisposition rather than factors of socialization. Socialization is probably a much stronger explanation for the major differences in crime rates that exist between men and women. As Bartol and Bartol explain:

> Traditionally, the social training of males and females has been very different...Even today, aggressive behavior in boys is encouraged, tolerated, or "understood"; in girls, it is condemned. Feminist literature, to its credit, makes a point of distinguishing between aggressiveness and assertiveness. The former implies a physical, "bullish" approach to problems; the latter implies a firm, competent, planful one (1986:238).

Research, in general, has ignored differences in the socialization process, which may be helpful in explaining why women commit less crime and men commit more. As long as researchers continue to treat men as the norm, important questions and issues regarding women and human beings in general are going to be ignored in theory, research, and policy. Both the concept of crime and the empirical method used to study crime cloak an androcentric (male-centered) value system blind to inequality and competing values. This may be one of the most important yet most ignored issues in the study of crime.

Some Epistemological Concerns of Feminism

Reiterating a point made by Dorothy Smith, Smart (1990:78) notes that "to direct research at women without revising traditional assumptions about methodology and epistemology can result in making women a mere addendum to the main project of studying men." It also leaves unchallenged the way men are studied. Thus the preclusion of women from the general discourse of the social sciences in general stems from the very way our methodologies have traditionally framed research questions and agendas.

One blatant example of this problem occurs in most attempts to do research regarding gender and/or racial equality and inequality. The very definition of equality that is operationalized to do the research is basically a white, Anglo-Saxon, male, liberal, version of equality. As MacKinnon (1987) points out, the norm is always the male gender. This leads to studies in the criminal justice system in which women are compared with men in favorable positions. Then the argument is made that women should be elevated to the status of men. In those situations where men are treated less favorably than women, the assumption is made that women's positions should be reduced to be equal with men's (Smart, 1990:79). Lahey refers to this phenomenon as "equality with a vengeance" (cited in Smart, 1990:79).

The conceptual bind is obvious: the standard that determines the outcome of the "objective" research is ultimately male-centered, which means the research is not objective.

Are feminists anti-science, then? No. Much of the work that has brought feminist issues (e.g., domestic abuse) to the public's attention is grounded in scientific research (see for an overview of feminist research Bartol and Bartol, 1986; Brown, 1990; Eisenberg and Lennon, 1983; Frodi, Macaulay and Thome, 1977; Gelsthorpe and Morris, 1990; Hoffman, 1977; Holstein, 1976; Murphy and Gilligan, 1980; Morash, 1983; Moyer, 1992; Naffine, 1987; Stanko, 1985; Schur, 1984; Widom, 1978). Some feminists suggest caution, however, in blindly espousing the goal of empiricism, which is to obtain "objective" and "true" knowledge (Smart, 1990). Harding (1986) suggests that a feminist empiricism is possible provided that the means of achieving "objective" knowledge are considered carefully in their appropriate epistemological context.

Harding (1986:162) suggests that feminist empiricism challenges the assumptions of traditional empiricism on three counts. First, feminist empiricists see the social identity of the observer as extremely relevant to research by virtue of the fact that the observer selects the scientific problem to be studied. They question the traditional empiricist's assumption that the observer is somehow independent from her/his research. Second, feminists question the ability of traditional scientific methodology to eliminate androcentric biases precisely because of its inability to detect them. Finally, "it challenges the belief that science must be protected from politics" (Harding, 1986:162). Harding explains:

> Objectivity is not maximized through value-neutrality — at least not in the way the traditional science discourses have construed these concepts. I have argued that it is only coercive values — racism, classism, sexism — that deteriorate objectivity; it is participatory values — antiracism, anticlassism, antisexism — that decrease the distortions and mystifications in our culture's explanations and understandings.

Why would an oppressed group of people trying to explain their oppression want to claim value neutrality when the circumstances that they find themselves in are not value neutral? This would be tantamount to using the weapons forged by their oppressors to cut their own throats. For example, attempts by researchers to explain oppression and discrimination of women by comparing them to men makes the assumption that men are the epitome of equality. These researchers assume that the measure of fairness and equality is the way men treat men. Thus, if women are being equally treated, they are being treated like men. The problem with this is that women's conceptions of equality and fairness are precluded from the assessment altogether. The male discourse monopolizes the concept of equality using its own standard to judge whether women are in fact "objects" of discrimination. In short, there is no value neutrality, only an androcentric value system claiming itself to be value neutral.

One of the major projects of what is referred to as standpoint feminism is to acknowledge the experience of women's oppression (Harding, 1986). Smart (1990:80) explains:

> Feminist experience is achieved through a struggle against oppression; it is therefore argued to be more complete and less distorted than the perspective of the ruling group of men. A feminist standpoint then is not just the experience of women, but of women reflexively engaged in struggle (intellectual and political). In this process it is argued that a more accurate or fuller version of reality is achieved. This stance does not divide knowledge from values and politics but sees knowledge rising from engagement.

The feminist perspective requires this understanding before any further discussion of feminist concerns can be undertaken.

The history of women has been one of objectification and subjugation which has manifested itself in the social and legal treatment of women as sexual objects and reproductive property of a patriarchal state. For example, why does a female rape victim have to prove her innocence in a court of law? Can we possibly believe our courts of law are really value neutral? Research has for a very long time ignored the degrading experience that women have undergone in the courts, especially regarding rape, sexual assault, and wife abuse. A standpoint feminist seeks to create a unitary reality where women's experience is integrated into the general operating discourse of society.

A more radical feminist position, referred to as feminist postmodernism, argues against any attempt at constructing a general integrative discourse. Feminist postmodernism sees truth claims, or in this case a monistic (singular) conception of general discourse, as creating power relations which inevitably oppress and subjugate. Attempting to express human experience through one voice, no matter how benevolent that voice is, will always require the silencing of many other voices. Thus the aim of feminist postmodernism, according to Smart (1990:82), "becomes the deconstruction of truth and analysis of the power effects which claims to truth entail." Feminism from a postmodernism perspective becomes a "multiplicity of resistance."

Feminism as an epistemological framework, then, does not contain an inclusive set of values that provide a definitive structure to confront sociopsychological problems. This has been a difficult point for many to understand precisely because they are operating in an androcentric value system that dictates a monistic conception of reality. Feminists on the other hand, have learned through a long history of oppression that people suffer different fates and have different problems. Accordingly, trying to construct a monistic feminist discourse would be contrary to the feminist empistemological project of acknowledging oppression in general, and specifically the oppression of women's diverse experiences.

Feminist Teachings On Crime And Justice

In not espousing any one value system, feminism espouses many values. If some of these values were put into practice many of them would lead to major changes in criminal justice policy. To achieve a healthy system of justice requires that we find what is destructive and repulsive about our current system and reinvent or replace it.

The overall health of the criminal justice system in the United States is not good. The United States criminal justice system has become more violent (police brutality), obtrusive (electronic monitoring), and oppressive (prison overcrowding) than ever before in its history. According to 1989 data, the United States ranked first in incarceration rates with 426 per 100,000; South Africa was second with 333 per 100,000 and the Soviet Union finished third with 268 per 100,000 people (Senna and Siegel, 1993:582). The United States in 1991 had 455 per 100,000 people incarcerated. South Africa had 311 per 100,000 (Senna and Siegel, 1993). Keep in mind that the U.S. often declares itself the leader of the free world. Since 1980 prison populations have more than doubled and as 1993 prison population ratio is the highest it has ever been in the history of this country (Senna and Siegel, 1993). In states like California, Colorado, and Michigan, prison populations have increased by 90 percent (Senna and Siegel, 1993). In sum, this surge in incarceration has led to prison overcrowding, which leads to idleness, increased danger, and outright hopelessness.

The general approach to crime in the U.S. has been to advocate a "get tough" stance on criminals. Politicians tout this rhetoric every election year and we accept it without question. The irony, however, is that each time we step up the war on crime, crime steps up its war on us. Not only do we promote violence with violence, we create a serious financial strain on other existing institutions designed to keep people from resorting to crime. The poor, education programs, and the overall economy suffer when inordinate amounts of money are invested in incarcerating literally millions of people.

It is our current mindset or "bonded rationality" which perpetuates this truly vicious cycle that many feminists call into question. Feminists question the increased reliance on the state to solve the very problems the state creates by relying on the same failing ideological beliefs, institutions, and war-oriented values. A feminist view of justice requires rethinking destructive ideologies, antiquated institutional practices and the use of dehumanizing values.

According to Harris (1991), a feminist perspective on justice includes consideration of three basic beliefs. In an effort to take the equality issue beyond the level of equal entitlement, Harris states that "all people have equal value" (1991:88) Harris claims that a feminist:

> insistence on equality in sexual, racial, economic, and all other types of relations stems from recognition that all humans are equally tied to the human condition, equally deserving of respect for their personhood, and equally worthy of survival and of access to those things that make life worth living (1991:88).

She stresses the importance of not construing this belief as a naive assertion that every human is identical. Rather, this belief acknowledges differences and diversity, but practices tolerance by giving "identical consideration to all human beings" (Harris, 1991:88). Harris contends that the goal of feminist justice is not just to obtain equal opportunity within the prevailing social structure but to change the prevailing structure to eliminate sexual, racial and economic injustices.

The second belief according to Harris (1991) entails adhering to felicity and harmony as values worth striving for. By this, Harris means that understanding the natural network on which we all depend for our basic needs, requires acknowledgement of important themes like "caring, sharing, nurturing, and loving" (1991:88). She notes that these themes are somewhat antithetical to current modes of valuing power, domination and hierarchy.

Harris is quick to point out that a value system rooted in power, domination and hierarchy quickly leads to division and exclusion, inevitably creating "resentment and revolt in various forms, which are then used to justify greater control" (1991:88). Witness the problem of urban poverty and violence.

This failure to perceive the interconnectedness and interdependence of human relationships leads to what Gearhart (1982) has referred to as objectification of the other. Gearhart writes:

> [t]hinking of myself as separate from another entity makes it possible for me to 'do to' that entity things that I would not 'do to' myself. But if I see all things as myself or empathize with all other things, then to hurt them is to do damage to me... [cited in Harris, 1991:91].

Before values like caring, sharing, and nurturing can become foundations for human organizations, the tendency to objectify others has to become something we are consciously aware of in our relationships. Once we become aware of our interconnectedness through the human condition and our social interdependence, this illusory objectification of one another seems quite irrational. Harris describes the third belief of feminist justice as an acceptance that "the personal is the political, which means that core values must be lived and acted upon in both public and private arenas" (1991:88). Her feminist version of justice rejects the notion that we should operate from a dualistic value system; that is, we should not have one value system for dealing in personal arenas and another value system for governing our actions in the world of politics and organizations. In other words, values that we practice in our family situations like empathy, compassion, and caring should be applied and affirmed outside of the home and integrated into the wider context of the social and political world (Harris, 191:88).

The feminist perspective on justice requires us to envision a new social reality. The first step in liberation is becoming aware of the fetters that confine us to a restricting social world and a constipated psychological existence. Feminists offer no single alternative; rather, they offer a world of many alternatives to deal with social problems and many modes of exploration for different versions of health and well-being. Feminists offer no one way to deal with crime and conflict, because they acknowledge openly that there is no one way to solve these problems. Part of escaping our current dilemma in the criminal justice system is to acknowledge the futility of unidimensional approaches to multidimensional problems.

THE CONCEPT OF PEACEMAKING

The underlying assumption of the peacemaking camp in criminology is also that the criminal justice system has failed in its mission to understand and solve crime problems. "The more we have reacted to crime, the farther we have removed ourselves from any understanding and any reduction of the problem" (Quinney, 1991:3). It is the failure of the criminal justice system that brings about the need for considering alternative visions of justice and conflict resolution. The goal of "[a] criminology of peacemaking, the nonviolent criminology of compassion and service, seeks to end suffering and thereby eliminate crime" (Quinney, 1991:4).

Peacemaking is a melding of three long-standing traditions in criminology. These traditions include religious traditions, feminist traditions and critical traditions (Pepinsky, 1991:299). According to Pepinsky, the most ostensible group of peacemaking oriented people are those who draw from some sort of religious tradition. He notes, "Religiously self-identified people cross all eight intellectual traditions which have emerged: academicians and theorists, activists and reformers, feminists, lawmakers, mediators, native traditionalists, people of color, and prisoners" (Pepinsky, 1991:300). The peacemaking tradition, then, draws on diverse perspectives, all of which cannot possibly be given adequate coverage in this section (for a comprehensive overview of peacemaking in criminology see Pepinsky and Quinney, 1991). As such, this section will focus only on some basic themes of peacemaking as explicated by Richard Quinney (1991:3-12).

Human Suffering

A peacemaking criminology begins with the assumption that all human beings suffer by virtue of their existence. Suffering is manifested in the existential anxiety and tension of our everyday physical and psychological reality, and our interpersonal relationships, which are often emotionally violent (Quinney, 1991:4). In addition, human suffering is everywhere – witness poverty, starvation, disease, and pollution. Even if by chance we were to bring about significant political and economic change, Quinney (1991) suggests that without a transformation from within each individual, large scale social changes are doomed to fail. Quinney's point is that in order to ameliorate human suffering in the world, we must begin by examining our own thoughts. Our social world is created from our thoughts – "we have constructed webs of meaning; and with these shared meanings we have constructed our interpersonal relations, our social structures, and our societies" (Quinney, 1991:4). Quinney goes on to suggest that "[t]he reconstruction of our existence — the end of suffering — thus begins by giving attention to the mind" (1991:4).

Quinney (1991) draws from Eastern wisdom, specifically Zen Buddhism, and suggests that our suffering is a direct result of our attachment to our ideas and thoughts about reality. He explains that most of these ideas and thoughts are deeply ingrained in us by our cultural conditioning. Cultural conditioning, then, shapes our perceptions of reality and limits our awareness of potentiality. The Zen approach requires that we let go of this conditioning which shapes the way we think about the world and which provides us with the illusion that we are in control of the world. Zen masters refer to this letting go as "beginners mind" (Quinney, 1991:5). Suzuki teaches, "If your mind is empty, it is always ready for anything; it is open to everything. In the beginner's mind there are many possibilities; in the expert's mind there are few" (cited in Quinney, 1991:5).

Thus, in order to make peace, one must become aware of the ideas and thoughts that create self interested egos — the source of our suffering, according to Quinney (1991). Quinney (1991:5) writes:

> The higher wisdom, the awareness of reality, can be attained only with the loss of the conditioned ego and with the realization of the transcendental Self. In other words, the essence of our existence is the interpretation of ourselves with all things... Peace and harmony come with the awareness of the oneness of all things and the transcendence of this small self to the wholeness of reality. All of this is to be found outside of the abstracting interpretations of the rational mind.

According to Quinney (1991), when we become aware, we begin to practice ways of ending suffering.

Awareness, Compassion and Service

The path to awareness begins with an understanding that every action has a consequence, making true reality contingent and always in a state of flux (Quinney, 1991). Egocentric actions like greed and hatred ultimately produce consequences which tend to fuel greater suffering. True reality is the acknowledgment of nothingness — in true reality there is nothing that can be sought or gained. It is communion with the void that brings about the awareness that all human life is in the same condition and thus in need of compassion.

Awareness leads to an understanding of interrelationships rather than differences. As Quinney (1991) notes, peacemaking criminology is an attempt to avoid the traps and limitations of a pure positive scientific approach. He notes that after years of being trained in positive science an individual can become indifferent, unconcerned and impervious to feeling. The process of atomizing and analytically dissecting problems will eventually lead to the kind of mind which loses its ability to exercise empathy and compassion (Quinney, 1991). Quinney asserts that "[t]he compassionate mind is found beyond the boundaries of Western scientific rationality" (1991:7).

Compassion is felt, then, out of an understanding that develops in seeing interrelationships rather than differences. For instance, "[i]n compassion, the suffering of others is recognized out of one's own suffering, and the suffering is shared" (Quinney, 1991:9). To understand that all human beings suffer is to realize our connectedness with eachother. It is this mutual suffering and mutual understanding of this condition that brings about the inner knowledge of peace and subsequently the amelioration of human suffering.

The knowledge of peace begins with an understanding of human suffering. To bring this back to the problem of crime, Quinney notes that "crime is suffering and that the ending of crime is possible only with the ending of suffering" (1991:11). According to Quinney (1991), to relinquish crime and suffering requires that a true justice be established out of peace. True justice requires a transformation from suffering (i.e., ignorance, desire, hatred, greed etc.) to a state of inner peace by understanding the sources of our suffering. As we transform ourselves, we will inevitably transform our social, economic and political structures (Quinney, 1991:11-12). As Quinney points out, "[w]ithout peace within us and in our actions, there can be no peace in our results" (1991:12).

The peacemaking perspective provides an alternative way of viewing what peacemakers consider a very violent criminal justice system, a system which reacts to violence with violence in a futile attempt to make peace. The rationale of our criminal justice system is the same as that which guides us into war: that is, a philosophy of peace through strength (as measured by physical force), domination, and violence. The peacemaking perspective asks us to reconsider the success of this approach in dealing with crime and conflict. Is our society a safe and peaceful place to live? Can there be peace through violence? Has the war on crime prevented crime?

Current modes of peacemaking in criminology involve such activities as conflict resolution, mediation, and the outright abolition of practices like incarceration and capital punishment. Other attempts at instilling a peacemaking consciousness entail raising awareness of the structural dimensions of society which condone the abuse of women and children. In addition to these dimensions of peacemaking there have also been attempts to instill a sense of community through concepts like community policing, neighborhood courts and sanctions that deal with resolution and restitution. All of these are attempts to undermine the violence that is created by entrusting justice to an abstract entity like the state, which is indifferent to individual suffering and human suffering in general — witness any bureaucratic criminal justice system.

The peacemaking perspective provides us with insight into our current problems of violence and high crime rates. Peacemaking suggests that our crime problems are a result of our own personal suffering and our failure to understand others' personal suffering. When we wage war against crime we merely contribute to more suffering, which in turn results in more violence and pushes us further away from our criminal justice system's stated goal, which is supposedly "to keep the peace." It is all too obvious that our criminal justice system has failed to keep the peace and has failed to provide a safe environment. It is this unquestionable failure which the peacemaking perspective attempts to bring to our attention by pointing out the blatant paradox in our criminal justice system's stated mission and its achievements (or lack thereof).

SUMMARY

The purpose of this chapter has been to introduce to the reader the transpersonal perspective as a viable alternative approach to studying crime. Unlike the other psychological perspectives we have discussed in this text, the transpersonal perspective looks at ways to achieve psychological health and well-being by challenging reified beliefs about the social construction of our reality. Transpersonal psychology inquires into the relationship between social structure and psychological well-being. It invites us to reconsider our tendencies to focus exclusively on the rational egoistic model of knowing by pointing to the limitation of reducing complexity to simplicity.

The transpersonal perspective creates an awareness that humans possess unlimited potential, and can reconstruct and recreate the world by becoming aware that our problems are mostly self-imposed limitations. With respect to criminology, this awareness translates into changing antiquated premises that lead to a vicious cycle of failing criminal justice policies. In addition, making malevolent assumptions about human nature encourages human beings to act and think malevolently. The transpersonal perspective is an attempt to look for human meaning beyond the egocentric level by expanding our knowledge of humankind to encompass other realms of experience which lie outside of the purely rational mode.

To investigate the possibilities for expanding experience and creating change in criminal justice, this chapter explored two different realms of knowing and acting. Each one of these realms explores oppression and alternative modes of existing in the world. The first realm we explored was feminism. We considered perceptions of female crime, feminist epistemology concerns, oppression, justice, and issues of social health and well-being.

The other epistemological realm with concerns parallel to the transpersonal perspective is peacemaking. This section provided a cursory overview of some underlying themes of peacemaking criminology and provided some of the practical strategies being attempted to try to resist violent approaches to crime and justice problems.

Taken together, these three approaches provide us with alternative visions of reality. These perspectives remind us that we are not immutable automatons, rather we are creative beings whose potential for changing unfavorable circumstances is basically unlimited. Furthermore, true justice can only come about when human suffering and oppression ends and is no longer perpetuated by our social, economic, and political institutions.

References

Abrahamsen, D. 1960. *The Psychology of Crime*. New York: Columbia University Press.

Adler, F. 1975. *Sisters in Crime: The Rise of the New Female Criminal*. New York: McGraw Hill.

Ahlstrom, W.M., and R.J. Havinghurst (1971). *400 Losers*. San Francisco: Jossey-Bass.

Ahlstrom, W.M. and R.T. Havinghurst (1971). *400 Losers.*. San Francisco, CA.: Jossey Bass.

Aichhorn, A. 1935. *Wayward Youth*. New York: The Viking Press.

Akers, R.L. 1977. *Deviant Behavior: A Social Learning Approach (2nd ed.)*. Belmont, CA: Wadsworth.

Akers, R.L. 1985. *Deviant Behavior: A Social Learning Approach* (3rd ed.). Belmont, CA: Wadsworth.

Alexander, F. and W. Healey. 1935. *Roots of Crime*. New York: Knopf.

Allport, G.W. 1937. *Personality: A Psychological Interpretation*. New York: Holt.

Allport, G.W. 1968. *The Person in Psychology*. Boston: Beacon.

Allsopp, J.F. 1976. Criminality and Delinquency. In H.J. Eysenck & G.D. Wilson (Eds.), *A textbook of human psychology*. Baltimore: University Park Press.

Atkinson, R.L., R.C. Atkinson and E.R. Hilgard. 1981. *Introduction to Psychology*, (8th ed.). New York: Harcourt Brace Jovanovich, Inc.

Bandura, A. 1962. "Social Learning Through Imitation." In M.R. Jones (Ed.), *Nebraska Symposium on Morivation*. Lincoln: University of Nebraska Press.

Bandura, A. 1973. *Aggression: A Social Learning Analysis*. Englewood Cliffs, N.J.: Prentice-Hall.

Bandura, A. 1977. *Social Learning Theory*. Englewood Cliffs, N.J.: Prentice-Hall.

Bandura, A. 1983. Psychological Mechanisms of Aggression. In R. G. Geen and E.I. Donnerstein (Eds.), *Aggression: Theoretical and Empirical Reviews* (Vol. 1). New York: Academic Press.

Bandura, A. 1986 [1979]. The Social Learning Perspective: Mechanisms of Aggression. In Hans Toch (Ed.), *Psychology of Crime & Criminal Justice.* Prospect Heights, IL: Waveland Press.

Bandura, A., D. Ross, and S.A. Ross. 1961. Transmission of Aggression through Imitation of Aggressive Models. *Journal of Abnormal Social Psychology* 66:3-11.

Bandura, A., D. Ross, and S.A. Ross. 1963. Vicarious Reinforcement and Imitative Learning. *Journal of Abnormal Social Psychology* 67:601-607.

Bandura, A., and R.H. Walters. 1963. *Social Learning and Personality Development.* New York: Holt, Rinehart & Winston.

Baron, R.A. 1977. *Human Aggression.* New York: Plenum Press.

Bartol, C.R., and A.M. Bartol. 1986. *Crimnal Behavior: A Psychosocial Approach.* Englewood Cliffs, New Jersey: Prentice-Hall.

Bartol, C.R. and H.A. Holanchock. 1979. "A Test of Eysenck's Theory of Criminality on an American Prisoner Population." *Criminal Justice and Behavior* 6:245-249.

Beccaria, C. 1963 (1764). On Crimes and Punishments. New York: Bobbs-Merril.

Becker, H.S. 1963. Outsiders. New York: Free Press.

Belenky, M.F., B.M. Clinchy, N.R. Goldberger, and J.M. Tarule. 1986. *Women's Ways of Knowing.* New York: Basic Cooks, Inc.

Bennet, T. 1986. "A Decision Making Approach to Opioid Addiction." In D.B. Cornish and R.V. Clarke (Eds.), *The Reasoning Criminal: Rational Choice Perspective on Offending.* New York: Springer-Verlag.

Bentham, J. 1948. *An Introduction to the Principles of Morals and Legislation.* Oxford: Blackwell.

Blalock, H.M. 1982. *Conceptualization and Measurement in the Social Sciences.* Beverly Hills, CA: Sage.

Blumstein, A., and J. Cohen. 1979. "Estimation of Individual Crime Rates from Arrest Records." *Journal of Crimnal Law and Criminology* 70:561-585.

Brown, B. 1990. "Reassessing the Critique of Biologism." In L. Gelsthorpe and A. Morris (Eds.), *Feminist Perspectives in Criminology.* Philadelphia: Open University Press.

Brown, N.O. 1959. *Life Against Death: The Psychoanalytical Meaning of History.* New York: Vintage Books.

Burgess, R.L., and R.L. Akers 1966. "A Differential Association Reinforcement Theory of Criminal Behavior." *Social Problems* 14: 128-147.

Camus, A. 1961. *The Myth of Sisyphus.* New York: Vintage Books.

Capra, F. 1983. *The Turning Point: Science, Society, and the Rising Culture.* New York: Bantam Books.

Carrol, J.S. 1982. "Committing a Crime. The Offenders Decision." In V. J. Konecni and E. B. Ebbesen (Eds.), *The Criminal Justice System: A Social-Psychological Analysis.* Oxford: Freeman.

Carrol, J.S., and F. Weaver. 1986. "Shoplifters Perceptions of Crime Opportunities: A Process-tracing study." In D. B. Cornish and R. V. Clarke (Eds.), *The Reasoning Criminal: Rational Choice Perspective on Offending.* New York: Springer-Verlag.

Chapman, J. R. 1980. *Economic Realities and the Female Offender.* Lexington, MS: Lexington

Books.
Chomsky, N. 1959. "Verbal Behavior (a review)." *Language* 35:26-58.
Clarke, R.V., and D.B. Cornish. 1985. "Modeling Offenders' Decisions: A Framework for Research and Policy." In M. Tonry and N. Morris (Eds.), *Crime and Justice: An Annual Review of Research*, Vol 6. Chicago: University of Chicago Press.
Clinard, M.B. 1974. *Sociology of Deviant Behavior* (4th ed.), New York: Holt Rinehart and Winston, Inc.
Cook, P.J. 1980. "Research in Criminal Deterrence: Laying the Groundwork for the Second Decade." In N. Morris and M Torny (Eds.), *Crime and Justice: An Annual Review of Research*, Vol 2. Chicago: University of Chicago Press.
Corey, G. 1991. *Theory and Practice of Counseling and Psychotherapy*, (4th ed.). Pacific Grove, CA: Brooks/Cole Publishing Company.
Cornish, D.B. 1978. "Gambling: A Review of the Literature and Its Implications for Policy and Research." Home Office Research Study, no. 42. London: HMSO.
Cornish D.B., and R.V. Clarke (Eds.). 1986. *The Reasoning Criminal: Rational Choice Perspective on Offending*. New York: Springer-Verlag.
Cortes, J.B., and F.M. Gatti. 1972. *Delinquency and Crime: A Biopsychosocial Approach*. New York: Seminar Press.
Cressey, D.R. 1962. The Development of a Theory: Differential Association. In M.E. Wolfgang, L. Savitz, & N. Johnston (Eds.), *The Sociology of Crime and Delinquency*, (pp.43-54). New York: John Wiley & Sons.
Cusson, M., and P. Pinsonneault. 1986. "The Decision to Give Up Crime." In D.B. Cornish and R.V. Clarke (Eds.), *The Reasoning Criminal: Rational Choice Perspective on Offending*. New York: Springer-Verlag.
Daly, K. 1989. "Neither Conflict nor Labeling nor Paternalism will Suffice: Intersections of Race, Ethnicity and Family in Criminal Court Decisions." *Crime and Delinquency* 35:136-168.
Darwin, C. 1958 (1859). *The Origin of Species*. New York: Penguin Books.
Denno, D. 1985. "Sociological and Human Developmental Explanations of Crime: Conflict or Consensus." *Criminology* 23:711-741.
Dollard, J., N.E. MIller, L.W. Doob, O.H. Mowrer, and R.R. Sears. 1939. *Frustration and Aggression*. New Haven: Yale University Press.
Dostoevsky, F. 1957. *The Brothers Karamazov*. New York: New American Library.
Dostoevsky, F. 1961. *Notes From Underground: White Nights: The Dream of a Ridiculous Man: and Selections from The House of the Dead*. New York: New American Library.
Driscoll, L.N. 1992. "An Assessment of the "General" Theory of Crime Proposed by Gottfredson and Hirschi (1990)." A Dissertation, Indiana Univeristy of Pennsylvania.
Eisenberg, N., and R. Lennon. 1983. "Sex Differences in Empathy and Related Capacities." *Psychological Bulletin* 94:100-131.
Eysenck H.J. 1948. *Dimensions of Personality*. London: Routledge & Kegan Paul.
Eysenck, H.J. 1977. *Crime and Personality*, (2nd ed.). London: Routledge & Kegan Paul.

Eysenck, H.J. 1984. "Crime and Personality." In D.J. Muller, D.E. Blackman, and A.J. Chapman (Eds.), *Psychology and Law*. Chichester, England: John Wiley & Sons Ltd.

Farrel, R.A. 1989. "Cognitive Consistency in Deviance Causation: A Psychological Elaboration of an Integrated Systems Model." In S.F. Messner, M.D. Krohn, and A.E. Liska (Eds.), *Theoretical Integration in the Study of Deviance and Crime: Problems and Prospects*. New York: State University of New York Press.

Farrington, D., L.E. Ohlin, and J.Q. Wilson. 1986. *Understanding and Controlling Crime: Towards a New Strategy*. New York: Springer-Verlag.

Farrington, D.P., L. Biron, and M. LeBlanc. 1982. "Personality and Delinquency in London and Montreal." In J. Gunn and D.P. Farrington (Eds.), *Abnormal offenders, Delinquency, and the Criminal Justice System*. Chichester, England: John Wiley.

Feldman, M.P. 1977. *Criminal Behaviour: A Psychological Analysis*. London: John Wiley.

Feeney, F. 1986. "Robbers as Decision-makers." In D.B. Cornish and R.V. Clarke (Eds.), *The Reasoning Criminal: Rational Choice Perspective on Offending*. New York: Springer-Verlag.

Frazier, A.M. 1970. *Readings In Eastern Religious Thought: Buddhism*. Philadelphia, PA: The Westminster Press.

Frankl, V.E. 1963. *Man's Search For Meaning: An Introduction To Logotherapy*. New York: Washington Square Press.

Freedman, B.J., L. Rosenthal, C.P. Schlundt, and R.M. McFall. 1978. "A Social-Behavioral Analysis of Skill Deficits in Delinquent and Non-delinquent Adolescent Boys." *Journal of Consulting and Clinical Psychology* 46 (1):448-462.

Freud, S. 1946 (1918). *Totem and Taboo*. New York: Vintage Books.

Freud, S. 1949. *An Outline of Psycho-Analysis*. New York: W.W. Norton & Company.

Freud, S. 1959. *Beyond the Pleasure Principle*. New York: Bantam Books.

Freud, S. 1960. *The Ego and the Id*. New York: W.W. Norton & Company.

Freud, S. 1961a. *Civilization and its Discontents*. New York: W.W. Norton & Company.

Freud, S. 1961b. *The Future of an Illusion*. New York: W.W. Norton & Compnay.

Freud, S. 1965. *The Psychopathology of Everyday Life*. New York: W.W. Norton & Company.

Friedlander, K. 1947. *Psychoanlytic Approach to Delinquency*. New York: International Universities Press.

Frodi, A., J. Macaulay, and P. Thome. 1977. "Are Women Always Less Aggressive than Men? A Review of the Experimental Literature." *Psychological Bulletin* 84:634-660.

Fromm, E. 1969 (1941). *Escape From Freedom*. New York: Holt, Rinehart & Winston, Inc.

Gagne, E.D. 1985. *The Cognitive Psychology of Social Learning*. Boston, MA: Little, Brown and Company.

Galliher, J.F. 1991. "The Willie Horton Fact, Faith and Commonsense Theory of Crime." In H. E. Pepinsky and R. Quinney (Eds.), *Criminology As Peace Making*. Bloomington, Indiana: Indiana University Press.

Gaylord, M.S. and J.F. Galliher 1988. *The Criminology of Edwin Sutherland*. New Brunswick, NJ: Transaction Books.

Gearhart, S.M. 1982. "The Future—If There Is One—Is Female." In Pam McAllister (ed.),

Reweaving the Web of Life: Feminsim and Nonviolence. Philadelphia: New Society Pub.
Gelsthorpe, L., and A. Morris (Eds.). 1990. *Feminist Perspectives in Criminology*. Philadelphia: Open University Press.
Gibbons, D.C. 1982. *Society, Crime and Criminal Behavior*, (4th ed.). Englewood Cliffs, NJ: Prentice Hall.
Gibbs, J.P. 1987. "The State of Criminological Theory." *Criminology* 25:821-840.
Gibbs, J.J., and P.L. Shelly. 1982. "Life in the Fast Lane: A Retrospective View by Commercial Thieves." *Journal of Research in Crime and Delinquency* 19:299-330.
Gilligan, C. 1982. *In a Different Voice: Psychological Theory and Women's Development*. Cambridge: Harvard University Press.
Glueck, S., and E. Glueck. 1950. *Unvraveling Juvenile Delinquency*. New York: Harper & Row.
Glueck, S., and E. Glueck. 1979. "Unraveling Juvenile Delinquency." In J. Jacoby (Ed.), *Classics of Criminology*. Oak Park, Illinois: Moore Publishing Co.
Goddard, H.H. 1912. *The Kallikak Family, A Study in the Heredity of Feeble-Mindedness*. New York: Macmillan.
Goodson, F. E. and G. A. Morgan. 1976. "Evaluation of Theory" In M.H. Marx and F.E. Goodson (Eds.), *Theories in Contemporary Psychology*. New York: Macmillan Publishing Co.
Gordon, R. 1976. "Pravalence: The Rare Datum in Delinquency Measurement and its Implications for the Theory of Delinquency." In M.W. Klein (ed.), *The Juvenile Justice System*. Beverly Hills, CA: Sage.
Goring, C. 1972 (1913). *The English Convict. A Statistical Study*. Montclair, NJ: Patterson Smith.
Gossop, M.R. and I. Kristjansson. 1977. "Crime and Personality." *British Journal of Criminology* 17:264-273.
Gottfredson M.R., and T. Hirschi (Eds.). 1987. *Positive Criminology*. Newbury Park, CA: Sage Publications.
Gottfredson M.R., and T. Hirschi. 1990. *A General Theory of Crime*. Stanford, CA: Stanford University Press.
Gould, S.J. 1981. *The Mismeasure of Man*. New York: W.W. Norton & Company.
Grasmich, H.G., C.R. Tittle, R.J. Bursik, and B.J. Arneklev. 1993. "Testing the Core Empirical Implications of Gottfredson and Hirschi's Theory of Crime." *Journal of Research in Crime and Delinquency*. 30:5-29.
Gribbin, J. 1984. *In Search of Schrodinger's Cat: Quantum Physics and Reality*. New York: Bantam Books.
Groves, B.W., and M.J. Lynch. 1990. "Reconciling Structural and Subjective Approaches to the Study of Crime." *Journal of Research in Crime and Delinquency* 27(4):348-375.
Groves, B.W. and D.H. Galaty. 1993. "Freud, Foucault, and Social Control, In G.R. Newman, M.J. Lynch, and D.H. Galaty (Eds.), *Discovering Criminology From W. Byron Groves*. New York: Harrow and Heston Publishers.
Hagan, F.E. 1986. *Introduction to Theories, Methods, and Criminal Behavior*. Chicago: Nelson Hall.

Halsbach, K. 1979. "Differential Reinforcement Theory Examined." *Criminology*, 17:217-229.

Harding, S. 1986. *The Science Question in Feminism*. Ithaca: Cornell University Press.

Harris, M.K. 1991. "Moving into the New Millennium: Toward a Feminist Vision of Justice." In H. E. Pepinsky and R. Quinnney, *Criminology as Peacemaking*. Bloomington, Indiana: Indiana University Press.

Heilbrun, A.B. 1979. "Psychopathy and Violent Crime." *Journal of Consulting and Clinical Psychology* 47:509-516.

Heilbrun, A.B. 1982. "Cognitive Models of Criminal Violence Based Upon Intelligence and Psychopathy Levels." *Journal of Consulting and Clincial Psychology* 50:546-557.

Higins, J.P., and A.P. Thies. 1981. "Social Effectivenss and Problem-Solving Thinking of Reformatory Inmates." *Journal of Offender Counselling Services and Rehabilitation* 5:93-98.

Hirschi, T. 1969. *Causes of Delinquency*. Berkeley, CA: University of California Press.

Hirschi, T., and M.J. Hindelang. 1977. "Intelligence and Delinquency." *American Sociological Review* 42:571-587.

Hoffman, M. 1977. "Sex Differences in Empathy and Related Behaviors." *Psychological Bulletin* 84:712-722.

Hollin, C.R. 1989. *Psychology and Crime: An Introduction to Criminological Psychology*. London, England: Routledge.

Holstein, C. 1976. "Irrevisible, Stepwise Sequence in the Development of Moral Judgment: A Longitudinal Study of Males and Females." *Child Development* 47:51-61.

Hooton, E.A. 1939. *The American Criminal: An Anthropological Study*. Cambridge, MA: Harvard University Press.

Horney, K. 1945. *Our Inner Conflicts*. New York: W.W. Norton & Company.

Husserl, E. 1975. *Ideas: General Introduction to Pure Phenomenology*. New York: Collier.

Jacoby, J.E. 1977. "Review of Yochelson and Samenow's The Criminal Personality, Vol 1." *Journal of Criminal Law and Criminology* 68:314-315.

James, J. 1976. "Motivations for Entrance into Prostitution." In L. Crites (ed.), *The Female Offender*. Lexington, MA: Lexington Books.

Jeffery, C.R. 1965. "Criminal Behavior and Learning Theory." *The Journal of Criminal Law, Criminology, and Police Science* 56:294-300.

Johnson, R.N. 1972. *Aggression in Man and Animals*. Philadelphia: W. B. Saunders Company.

Jones, E. 1953. *The Life and Work of Sigmund Freud: The Formative Years and the Great Discoveries* (Vol. 1). New York: Basic Books.

Katz, J. 1988. *Seductions of Crime: The Moral and Sensual Attractions of Doing Evil*. New York: Basic Books.

Kaufmann, W. 1975. *Existentialism from Dostoevsky to Sartre*. New York: New American Library.

Kavaler, L. 1965. *Mushrooms, Molds, and Miracles: A Fascinating Journey into the Strange Realm of the Fungi—Man's Greatest Friends and Deadliest Foes*. New York: New American Library.

Keane, C., P.S. Maxim, and J.J. Teevan. 1993. "Drinking and Driving, Self-control, and Gender: Testing a General Theory of Crime." *Journal of Research in Crime and Delinquency*. 30:30-46.

REFERENCES

Kierkegaard, S. 1980. *The Concept of Anxiety: A Simple Psychologically Orienting Deliberation on the Dogmatic Issue of Hereditary Sin.* Edited by R. Thomte and A. B. Anderson. Princeton, New Jersey: Princeton University Press.

Kohlberg, L. 1969. "Stage and Sequence: The Cognitive-Developmental Approach to Socialization." In D. A. Goslin (Ed.), *Handbook of Socialization Theory and Research.* Chicago: Rand McNally.

Kohlberg, L. 1973. "Implications of Developmental Psychology for Education: Examples from Moral Development." *Educational Psychologist* 10:2-14.

Kozielecki, J. 1982. *Psychological Decision Theory.* Boston: Reidel.

Kuhn, T.S. 1970 [1962]. *The Structure of Scientific Revolutions.* Chicago, IL: University of Chicago Press.

Kumchy, C. and L.A. Sayer. 1980. "Locus of Control and Delinquent Adolescent Populations." *Psychological Reports* 46:1307-1310.

Liebert, R.M., and M.D. Spiegler. 1970. *Personality: An Introduction to Theory and Research.* Homewood, IL: The Dorsey Press.

Liska, A.E., M.D. Krohn, and S.F. Messner. 1989. "Strategies and Requisties for Theoretical Integration in the Study of Crime and Deviance." In S. F. Messner, M.D. Krohn, and A.E. Liska (eds.), *Theoretical Integration in the Study of Deviance and Crime: Problems and Prospects.* Albany, New York: State University of New York Press.

Loeber, R., and T. Dishion. 1983. "Early Predictors of Male Delinquency: A review." *Psychological Bulletin* 94: 68-99.

Lombroso, C. 1863. *Criminal Man (L'Uomo Delinquente).* Turin, Italy: Fratelli Bocca, 5th edition. Lombroso, C. 1972 [1911]. *Criminal man. (L' Uomo Delinquente)* (Lombroso-Ferrero, Trans.) Montclair, NJ: Patterson Smith.

Lynch, M.J., and W.B. Groves. 1989. *A Primer in Radical Criminology,* (2nd ed.). New York: Harrow and Heston, Publishers.

MacKinnon, C. 1987. *Feminism Unmodified: Discourses on Life and Law.* Cambridge, MA: Harvard University Press.

Maddi, S.R. 1980. *Personality Theories. A Comparative Analysis,* (4th ed.). Homewood, IL: Dorsey Press.

Mannheim, H. 1965. *Comparative Criminology.* Boston: Houghton Mifflin.

Martin, R. 1985. "Perceptions of Self and Significant Others in Assaultive and Nonassaultive Criminals." *Journal of Police and Criminal Psychology* 1:2-13.

Martin, R. 1993. "Transpersonal Psychology and Criminological Theory: Rethinking the Paradigm." Forthcoming, *Journal of Crime and Justice,* Fall.

Martin, R., R.J. Mutchnick, and T.W. Austin. 1990. *Criminological Thought: Pioneers Past and Present.* New York: Macmillan Publishing Company.

Marx, M.H., and F.E. Goodson. (Eds.), 1976. *Theories in Contemporary Psychology.* New York: Macmillan Publishing Co.

Marx, M.H. 1976. "Formal Theory." in M.H. Marx and F.E. Goodson (Eds.), *Theories in Contemporary Psychology.* New York: Macmillan Publishing Co.

Massey, R.F. 1981. *Personality theories: Comparisons and syntheses.* New York: D. Van Nostrand Company.

Matza, D. 1964. *Delinquency and Drift.* New York: Wiley.

May, R. 1969. *Love and Will.* New York: W. W. Norton & Co.

Megargee, E.I. 1972. *The Psychology of Violence and Aggression.* (Reprint from a Report Prepared for the National Commission on the Causes and Prevention of Violence.) Morristown, NJ: General Learning Press.

Menard, S., and B. Morse. 1984. "A Structuralist Critique of IQ-Delinquency Hypothesis: Theory and Evidence." *American Journal of Sociology* 89:1347-1378.

Miller, E. M. 1986. *Street Woman.* Philadelphia: Temple University Press. Miller, G. A. 1962. *Psychology: The Science of Mental Life.* New York: Harper & Row.

Miller, G.A. 1962. *Psychology: The Science of Mental Life.* New York: Harper and Rowe.

Mischel, W. 1973. "Toward A Cognitive Social Learning Reconceptualization of Personality." *Psychological Review*, 80:252-283.

Mischel, W. 1979. "On the Interface of Cognition and Personality: Beyond the Person-Situation Debate." *American Psychologist* 34:740-754.

Morash, M. 1983. "An Explanation of Juvenile Delinquency: The Integration of Moral-Reasoning Theory and Sociological Knowledge." In W.S. Laufer and J.M. Day (Eds.), *Personality Theory, Moral Development, and Criminal Behavior.* Lexington, MA: Lexington Books.

Moyer, K.E. 1973. "The Physiological Inhibition of Hostile Behavior." In J. F. Knutson (Ed.), *The Control of Aggression.* Chicago: Aldine.

Moyer, I.L. 1992. *The Changing Roles of Women in the Criminal Justice System: Offenders, Victims, and Professionals,* (2nd ed). Prospect Heights, IL: Waveland Press.

Murphy, J.M., and C. Gilligan. 1980. "Moral Development in Late Adolescence and Adulthood: A Critique and Reconstruction of Kohlberg's Theory." *Human Development* 23:77-104.

Naffine, N. 1987. *Female Crime: The Construction of Women in Criminology.* Winchester, MA: Allen & Unwin.

Newman, G.R. 1979. *Understanding Violence.* New York: J. B. Lippincott Company.

Nietzel, M.T. 1979. *Crime and its Modification: A Social Learning Perspective.* Oxford: Pergamon.

Nietzsche, F. 1956. *The Birth of Tragedy: The Genealogy of Morals.* New York: Anchor Books.

Nietzsche, F. 1966. *Beyond Good and Evil.* New York: Vintage Books.

Passingham, R.E. 1972. "Crime and Personality: A Review of Eysenck's Theory." In V.D. Nebylitsyn and J.A. Gray (Eds.), *Biological Bases of Individual Behavior.* New York: Academic Press.

Peat, D.F. 1991. *The Philospher's Stone: Chaos, Synchronicity, and the Hidden Order of the World.* New York: Bantam Books.

Pepinsky, H.E. 1991. "Peacemaking in Criminology and Criminal Justice." In H.E. Pepinsky and R. Quinney (Eds.), *Criminology as Peacemaking.* Bloomington, IN: Indiana University Press.

REFERENCES

Pepinsky, H.E., and R. Quninney (Eds.). 1991. *Criminology as Peacemaking*. Bloomington, IN: Indiana University Press.

Pfuhl E.H. 1986. *The Deviance Process*. Belmont, CA: Wadsworth.

Piaget, J. 1952. *The Origins of Intelligence in Children*. New York: International Universities Press.

Platt, J.J., W. Scura, and J.R. Hannon. 1973. "Problem-Solving Thinking of Youthful Incarcerated Heroin Addicts." *Journal of Community Psychology* 1:278-281.

Quinney, R. 1991. "The Way of Peace: On Crime, Suffering and Service." In H.E. Pepinsky and R. Quinney (Eds.), *Criminology as Peacemaking*. Bloomington, IN: Indiana University Press.

Redl, F and H. Toch. 1986 [1979]. "The Psychoanalytic Perspective." In Hans Toch (ed.)., *Psychology of Crime & Criminal Justice*. Prospect, Heights, IL: Waveland Press, Inc.

Reiff, P. 1961. *Freud: The Mind of the Moralist*. Garden City, NJ: Doubleday Anchor Books.

Reich, W. 1970. *The Mass Psychology of Facism*. New York: Farrar, Straus & Giroux.

Rogers, C.R. 1963. Learning to be Free. In S.M. Farber and R.H.L. Wilson (Eds.), *Control of the Mind (Vol. 2): Conflict and Creactivity*. New York: McGraw-Hill.

Ross, R.R., and E.A. Fabino. 1985. *Time to Think: A Cognitive Model of Delinquency Prevention and Offender Rehabilitation*. Johnson City, TN: Institute of Social Science and Arts.

Rotter, J.B. 1954. *Social Learning and Clinical Psychology*. Englewood Cliffs, N.J.: Prentice-Hall.

Rotter, J.B. 1972. "Some Implications of A Social Learning Theory for the Practice of Psychotherapy." In J.B. Rotter, J. Chance, and F Phares (Eds.). *Applications of Social Learning Theory of Personality*. New York: Holt, Rinehart, & Winston.

Samenow, S.E. 1983. "Violence in Every Soul?" In W.S. Laufer J.M. Day (Eds.), *Personality Theory, Moral Development, and Criminal Behavior*. Lexinton, MA: Lexington Books.

Samenow, S.E. 1984. *Inside the Criminal Mind*. New York: Times Books.

Samuel, W. 1981. *Personality: Searching for the Source of Human Behavior*. New York: McGraw-Hill Book Company.

Sarte, J.P. 1968. *Being and Nothingness*. New York: Washington Square Press.

Schuessler, K., and D. Cressey. 1950. "Personality Characteristics of Criminals." *American Journal of Sociology* 55:476-484.

Schur, E.M. 1984. *Labeling Women Deviant: Gender, Stigma and Social Control*. New York: Random House.

Scroggs, J.R. 1985. *Key Ideas in Personality Theory*. New York: West Publishing Company.

Senna J.J., and L.J. Siegel. 1993. *Introduction to Criminal Justice*. St Paul, MN: West Publishing Company.

Sheldon, W.H., and S.S. Stevens. 1942. *The Varieties of Temperament*. New York: Harper & Row.

Sheldon, W.H., E.M. Hartl, and E. McDermott. 1949. *Varieties of Delinquent Youth*. New York: Harper & Brothers.

Shoham, S.G. 1979. *Salvation Through the Gutters: Deviance and Transcendence*. New York: Hemisphere Publishing Corporation.

Shoham, S.G. 1983a. *Sex As Bait: Eve, Casonova, and Don Juan*. New York: Queensland Press.

Shoham, S.G. 1983b. *The Violence of Silence*. London, England: Transaction Books.
Shoham, S.G. 1985. *Rebellion, Creativity, and Revelation*. Brunswick: Transaction Books.
Shoham, S.G., and G. Rahav. 1982. *The Mark of Cain* (2nd ed.). St Lucia, Queensland: University of Queensland Press.
Shoham, S.G., Z. Schwartzman, G. Rahav, R. Markowski, F. Chard, and A. Edelstein. 1987. "An Instrument to Diagnose Personality Types According to the Personality Theory of Shoham." *Medicine and Law*, 6:353-372.
Shoham S.G., and J Hoffman. 1991. *A Primer in the Sociology of Crime*. New York: Harrow and Heston.
Shoemaker, D.J. 1984. *Theories of Delinquency. An Examination of Explanations of Delinquent Behavior*. New York: Oxford University Press.
Siegel, L.J. 1989. Criminology. (3rd ed.), St. Paul, MN: West Publishing Company.
Simons, R.L. 1978. "The Meaning of the IQ-Delinquency Relationship." *American Sociological Review* 43:268-270.
Skinner, B.F. 1948. *Walden Two*. New York: Macmillan.
Skinner, B.F. 1953. *Science and Human Behavior*. New York Macmillan.
Skinner, B.F. 1980 [1971]. *Beyond Freedom and Dignity*. New York: Bantam Books.
Smart, C. 1979. "The New Female Criminal: Reality or Myth?" *British Journal of Criminology* 19:50.
Smart, C. 1990. "Feminist Approaches to Criminology or Postmodern Woman Meets Atavistic Man." In L. Gelsthorpe and A. Morris (Eds.), *Feminist Perspectives in Criminology*. Philadelphia: Open University Press.
Snarey, John. 1987. "A Question of Morality." *Psychological Bulletin*, 97:202-232.
Stanko, E.A. 1985. *Intimate Intrusions: Women's Experience of Male Violence*. New York: Routledge & Kegan Paul.
Stinchcombe, A.L. 1968. *Constructing Social Theories*. New York: Harcourt, Brace World.
Sunberg, N., and C. Keutzer. 1984. "Transpersonal Psychology I." In R.J. Corsini (Ed.), *Encyclopedia of Psychology*, Vol 3 (pp. 441-442). New York: John Wiley & Son.
Sutherland, E.H. 1939. *Principles of Criminology* (3rd ed.), Philadelphia: J. B. Lippincott Company.
Sutherland, E.H. 1947. *Principles of Criminology* (4th ed.), Philadelphia: J. B. Lippincott Company.
Sutherland, E.H. 1973. *Edwin H. Sutherland on Analyzing Crime*. Edited by K. Schuessler. Chicago: The University of Chicago Press.
Tannenbaum, D. 1977. "Research Studies of Personality and Criminality." *Journal of Crimnal Justice* 5:1-19.
Tappan, P. 1947. "Who is the Criminal?" *American Sociological Review* 12:97-102.
Taylor, I., P. Walton, and J. Young. 1973. *The New Criminology: For a Social Theory of Deviance*. London: Routledge & Kegan Paul Ltd.
Toch, H. 1969. *Violent Men: An Inquiry into the Psychology of Violence*. Chicago: Aldine Publishing Company

Toch, H. 1977. *Living in Prison the Ecology of Survival*. New York: Free Press.

Toch, H. 1986 [1979]. "The Psychology of Imprisonment." In H. Toch (Ed.), *Psychology of Crime and Criminal Justice*. Prospect Heights, Illinois: Waveland Press.

Toch, H. (Ed.). 1986 [1979]. *Psychology of Crime and Criminal Justice*. Prospect Heights, Illinois: Waveland Press.

Toch, H. 1987. "Supplementing the Positivistic Perspective." In M. Gottfredson and T. Hirschi (Eds.), *Positive Criminology*. Newbury Park, CA: Sage Publications.

Vold, G.B. and T.J. Benard. 1986. *Theoretical Criminology*, (3rd ed.). New York: Oxford University Press.

Waldo, G., and S. Dinitz. 1967. "Personality Attributes of the Criminal: An Analysis of Research Studies 1950-1965." *Journal of Research in Crime and Delinquency* 4:185-201.

Walsh, D.P. 1978. *Shoplifting: Controlling a Major Crime*. London: Macmillan.

Walsh, D.P. 1980. *Break-Ins: Burglary from Private Houses*. London: Constable.

Walsh, R.N., and F. Vaughan (Eds.). 1980. *Beyond Ego: Transpersonal Dimensions in Psychology*. Los Angeles: J. P. Tarcher, Inc.

Walsh, R.N., and F. Vaughan. 1980a. "Introduction: The Emergence of the Transpersonal Perspective." In R.N. Walsh and F. Vaughan (Eds.), *Beyond Ego: Transpersonal Dimensions in Psychology* (pp. 15-24). Los Angeles: J. P. Tarcher, Inc.

Walsh, R.N., and F. Vaughan. 1980b. "What is a Person?" In R.N. Walsh and F. Vaughan (Eds.), *Beyond Ego: Transpersonal Dimensions in Psychology* (pp. 53-62). Los Angeles: J. P. Tarcher, Inc.

Walsh, R.N., and F. Vaughan. 1984. "Transpersonal Psychology II. In R. J. Corsini (Ed.), *Encyclopedia of Psychology*, Vol 3 (pp. 442-444). New York: John Wiley & Sons.

Watson, J.B. 1913. Psychology as a Behaviorist Views It. *Psychlogical Review*, 20: 158-177.

Watson. J.B. 1924. *Behaviorism*. New York: People's Institute Publishing Company.

Walters, G.D., and T.W. White. "The Thinking Criminal: A Cogntive Model of Lifestyle Criminality." *Criminal Justice Research Bulletin* 4(4):1-10.

Widom, C.S. 1978. "An Empirical Classification of Female Offenders." *Criminal Justice and Behavior* 5:35-52.

Wilber, K. 1979. *No Boundary*. Boulder, CO: Shambala. Wilson, J.Q., and R.J. Herrnstein. 1985. *Crime and Human Nature: The Definitive Study of Causes of Crime*. New York: Simon & Schuster, Inc.

Wilson, J.W. and R.J. Herrnstein. 1985. *Crime and Human Nature: The Definitive Study of the Causes of Crime*. New York: Simon and Schuster.

Wolfgang, M.E., and F. Ferracuti. 1967. *The Subculture of Violence Towards an Integrated Theory in Criminology*. New York: Tavistock Publications.

Wolheim, R. 1971. *Sigmund Freud*. New York: The Viking Press.

Yochelson, S., and S.F. Samenow. 1976. *The Criminal Personality*, Vol 2. New York: Aronson.

Zohar, D. 1990. *The Quantum Self: Human Nature and Consciousness Defined by the New Physics*. New York: Quill/William Morrow.

Index

Adler, Freda 144
aggression
    acquisition mechanisms 78-80
    instigation mechanisms 80
    maintaining mechanisms 81-82
    psychoanalytical view of 29-30
Aichorn, August 24
Akers, Ronald 67-71,83
Allport, Gordon 35-37,137-138
ambiguity tolerance 104-105
ambivert 48-49
atavism 40
autonomic nervous system 48
    parasympathetic 49
    sympathetic 48-49
avoidance response 67

Bandura, Albert 65,71,75-82,88,94
Beccaria, Cesare 97
behaviorism 58
Bentham, Jeremy 97
Binet, Alfred 42-43
Binswanger, Ludwig 113-114
Brown, Norman 17,29,33
Buber, Martin 113
Burgess, Robert 67-71,83
California Personality Inventory (CPI) 43
central nervous system 48
Clarke, R.V. 106-109

classical conditioning 50,57-61,63,73,75,88
    conditioned reflex 60
    conditioned response 58,60
    conditioned stimulus 58
    unconditioned response 58,60
    unconditioned stimulus 58,60
classical learning theory 47
classical school 97
cognitive decision making models 106
cognitive psychology 90
cognitive social learing theory 94-96
conceptual box 3
conflict theory 84
consciousness 19
Cornish, D.B. 106-109
criminal decision making models 106-108
crime
    legal definition 4-6
    relativity of 5-6

Darwin, Charles 12,15
Dasien 113-114
differential association 68,82-87
differential association-reinforcement 67-68
differential reinforcement 65-67
Dinitz, Simon 44
disidentify 140-142

existential perspective 111-113,115,127,130-132

INDEX

Eysenck, Hans 47-51,57,59-61,78
   extraversion 47-49,51-52
   introversion 48
   neuroticism 48-49
   personality dimension 47
   psychotism 48
   stability 48

Farrell, Ronald 104-105
feminism 136,143-144
   epistemology 146-148
   justice 149-152
   postmodernism 148-149
Frankl, Victor 113-114
Freud, Sigmund 4,7-8,12,14,16-23,27-28,30-31,35,59,81
Friedlander, K. 25-26
Fromm, Erich 29
frustration-aggression hypothesis 30,80

Glueck, Eleanor 43,100
Gleuck, Sheldon 43,100
Goodson, F.E. 10,12-13
Goring, Charles 40
Gottfredson, Michael 44,53-54
Gould, Stephen 42

Heilbrun, A.B. 100-101
Herrnstein, Richard 51-53,71-73
Hippocrates 39
Hirschi, Travis 44,53-54
Hoffman, J. 4
Hooten, E.A. 40,45
Horney, Karen 26
humanistic psychology 135
Husserl, Edmund 115

intelligence 41,52,100
   criticism of 41-42

Jeffery, C.R. 65-68

Katz, Jack 112,127-132
   background factors 127,130-131
   foreground factors 127,130-131
   moral transcendance 128-129
Kohlberg, L. 92-93
   conventional morality 92
   postconventional morality 93
   preconventional morality 92
Kretschmer, Emil 45
Kuhn, Thomas 1-4

locus of control 102
Lombroso, Cesare 39-40

Maslow, Abraham 135
Marx, M.H. 8-9
May, Rollo 113-114
Minnesota Multiphasic Personality Inventory (MMPI) 43,100
Mischel, W. 94,96
Morgan, G.A. 10,12-13

National Crime Victim Survey (NCVS) 5
   problems with 5-6

open system 36
operant behavior perspective 4
operant conditioning 11,51,57,61-65,67-68,72-76,81,83,89
   interval schedule 64
   primary reinforcer 64
   punishment 63-67,69
   ratio schedule 63
   reinforcement 63-66,68-69
   secondary reinforcer 64
   variable interval schedule 64

pansexualism 17
paradigm
   definition of 2-3
   shifts 3
Pavlov, Ivan 57-58,60,63
personality tests 43
peacemaking 136,143,152-155
Pepinsky, H. 152
phenomenological perspective 111-112, 115,127,130-132
philosophical positivism 7
phrenology 39
Piaget, Jean 92
proprium 36
psychoanalysis 12,14
psychoanalytical perspective 4, 14, 35, 56, 62,90-91,112

ego 20-22,81
eros (life instinct) 17,20,33-34
historical development 15
id 20-22,59,81
oedipal complex 22,28-29
overdeveloped superego 27
parental influence 24-27
pathological guilt 27-28
pleasure principle 20
preconsciousness 19
reality principle 20-21
role of guilt 18
role of repression 18
role of unconsciousness 18
school influence 26
superego 22-23,81
thanatos (death instinct) 17,20,33-34
unconsciousness 18-19
underdeveloped superego 24
validity of 31-32
view of human nature 16-17,33
view of society 16
weak ego 25
psychology
historical development 1

Quinney, Richard 152-154

rational choice models 96,98
Reich, William 29
reticular activating system 48
Rotter, Julian 76-77,82,88,94,96

Samenow, S.F. 99-100
self-report data 5
problems with 5-6
Shoham, S.G. 4,112,115-123,125-127,130-132
mytho-empiricism 116
ontological dimensions of crime 123-125
personality dynamic 118-121
social dimension of crime 126
transcendental projects 122-123,125
Sheldon, William 44-45
Skinner, B.F. 4,7,12,61-64,67,83
social learning theory 57,71,75-78,80,82-83, 87-89,96
expectancy of reinforcement 76-77
external reinforcement 77
internal reinforcement 77
somatotyping 44-47
cerebrotonia 46
ectomorphic 45-46
endomorphic 45-46
mesomorphic 45-47,52
somatotonia 46
viscerotonia 45
Sutherland, Edwin 65,66-68,82-87
symbolic interactionism 84,96,98,104

Tappan, Paul 4,6
Thematic Appreciation Test (TAT) 43
theoretical explanation 8
theoretical perspective 6
definition of 4
theory
canonization of 10-11
deductive 7
definition of 8
evaluation of 9-10
inductive 7
scientific 7
Toch, Hans 30,103
trait perspective 36
cardinal 36
central 37
physiological 39-40
secondary 37
transpersonal psychology 134-141,143

Uniform Crime Report (UCR) 5-6
problems with 5

Vaughan, F. 138-141

Waldo, G 44
Walsh, R.N. 138-141
Watson, John 58-59,62,83
Wilson, James 51-53,71-73

Yochelson, S. 99-100